More Praise for *Pro-Voice*

"In a world where everyone forces you to chose a side around abortion, *Pro-Voice* challenges all of us to put empathy first and ideology second. Aspen Baker radically reframes our current culture war over abortion by putting stories first. By centering the voices of women, Baker clearly explains that actual conversation—not preaching or stonewalling—is the only way to move forward."
—**Latoya Peterson, feminist, activist, and owner and Editor,**
   Racialicious.com

"We've made great progress on tough social issues by sharing our stories authentically. *Pro-Voice* dives into that topic and makes it actionable. If you're an organizer, it's a must-read in 2015!"
—**Raven Brooks, Editor, Netroots Nation**

"Thank you, Aspen, for asking the global community to create an environment of compassionate pro-voice dialogue around this ubiquitous, incendiary issue. May this book birth the healing we all need."
—**Deborah Santana, author, philanthropist, and founder of Do a Little**

"The pro-voice movement Aspen Baker founded in Exhale is based on the idea that we are all storytellers, with the right to our own stories, specifically that every woman has the right to her own feelings about the experience of abortion, whatever they might be. As a journalist who writes about reproductive rights, I truly believe this approach is the only way to bridge a divide in this country that is putting women's lives in peril."
—**Liz Welch, award-winning journalist and coauthor of *The Kids Are All***
   Right* and *I Will Always Write Back

"In *Pro-Voice*, Aspen Baker shows us how to make America's abortion wars a relic of the past. Sharing and listening can heal old wounds and generate a new understanding and respect for this deeply personal issue."
—**US Congresswoman Gwen Moore**

"The best social and policy change begins with having discussion in the real world with real people. In this book, Aspen shows us a way to listen to women in a deeper way, creating a space for us to see the complexity of experiences with abortion. This is the kind of space that will help us reach across the divisions that often separate us and see the humanity in each other. Bravo, Aspen and pro-voice!"
—**Eveline Shen, MPH, Executive Director, Forward Together**

"We have less and less authentic space for dialogue in our country, yet Aspen Baker has taken the power of listening into the most contentious of territories, the abortion debate. She has shown that the stories that emerge when someone feels respected and safe enough to share them have the power to heal. We can choose to listen, and if we do, perhaps we can create a healthier society."
—**Joe Lambert, founder and Executive Director, Center for Digital Storytelling**

"The abortion debate—or rather, standoff—is one of the most polarizing in our polarized country. *Pro-Voice* creates humane connections across the passion-filled gulf that divides abortion conversations; then, as Jonathan Powell has also written recently, 'There is no conflict in the world that cannot be solved.' If that is not a reason for hope, what is?"
—**Michael Nagler, author of *The Search for a Nonviolent Future* and *The Nonviolence Handbook* and President, Metta Center for Nonviolence**

"In *Pro-Voice*, Aspen Baker raises a bold mandate that we hear people's abortion stories and imagines a world in which abortion is understood not through conflict but through empathy, regardless of one's politics. Baker shows, despite the loud rhetoric, that personal experiences with abortion are rarely spoken, and even more rarely are they compassionately heard. Proudly defying political categorization, *Pro-Voice* challenges everyone to step away from the fight in favor of deeper understanding. This is a most courageous and necessary book."
—**Marjorie Jolles, PhD, Associate Professor, Women's and Gender Studies, Roosevelt University**

"Aspen Baker's sharply insightful new book illuminates the refreshing—and groundbreaking—attitude she takes toward abortion, a stance that embraces the emotional complexity of women's abortion experiences and reveals the discussion's many gray areas that are so often obscured by political gamesmanship."
—**Martha Shane, filmmaker, *After Tiller***

"In this wise and compassionate book, Aspen Baker makes clear how strange it is that the people who battle over abortion policy rarely hear the stories of women who have actually had abortions. With sensitivity and insight, she shows that people's personal stories can transform the debate. *Pro-Voice* is smart, provocative, and, finally, heartening."
—**Francesca Polletta, Professor of Sociology, University of California, Irvine, and author of *It Was Like a Fever***

PRO-VOICE

PRO-VOICE

HOW TO KEEP LISTENING WHEN
THE WORLD WANTS A FIGHT

ASPEN BAKER

Berrett–Koehler Publishers, Inc.
a BK Currents book

Berrett-Koehler Publishers, Inc.
1333 Broadway, Suite 1000, Oakland, CA 94612-1921
Tel: (510) 817-2277   Fax: (510) 817-2278   www.bkconnection.com

ORDERING INFORMATION
Quantity sales. Special discounts are available on quantity purchases by corporations, associations, and others. For details, contact the "Special Sales Department" at the Berrett-Koehler address above.

Individual sales. Berrett-Koehler publications are available through most bookstores. They can also be ordered directly from Berrett-Koehler: Tel: (800) 929-2929; Fax: (802) 864-7626; www.bkconnection.com

Orders for college textbook/course adoption use. Please contact Berrett-Koehler: Tel: (800) 929-2929; Fax: (802) 864-7626.

Orders by U.S. trade bookstores and wholesalers. Please contact Ingram Publisher Services, Tel: (800) 509-4887; Fax: (800) 838-1149; E-mail: customer.service@ingrampublisherservices.com; or visit www.ingrampublisherservices.com/Ordering for details about electronic ordering.

Real people's voices and stories are included throughout Pro-Voice. Individuals may be referred to by their real full name, their real first name, or a pseudonym based on the person's preference. Real names are used unless noted otherwise.

Sales of Pro-Voice support Exhale, a 501(c)(3) designated public-benefit organization.

Berrett-Koehler and the BK logo are registered trademarks of Berrett-Koehler Publishers, Inc.

Printed in the United States of America

Berrett-Koehler books are printed on long-lasting acid-free paper. When it is available, we choose paper that has been manufactured by environmentally responsible processes. These may include using trees grown in sustainable forests, incorporating recycled paper, minimizing chlorine in bleaching, or recycling the energy produced at the paper mill.

LIBRARY OF CONGRESS CATALOGING-IN-PUBLICATION DATA
Baker, Aspen.
Pro-voice : how to keep listening when the world wants a fight / by
Aspen Baker. — First Edition.
    pages cm
Includes bibliographical references and index.
ISBN 978-1-62656-110-6 (pbk.)
1. Abortion—United States. 2. Abortion—Law and legislation—United States.
3. Pro-life movement—United States. 4. Pro-choice movement—United States. I. Title.
HQ767.5.U5B345 2015
362.1988'80973--dc23
                                    2015003264

FIRST EDITION
20 19 18 17 16 15   10 9 8 7 6 5 4 3 2 1

INTERIOR DESIGN: VJB/Scribe   PROOFREADER: Henrietta Bensussen
EDITOR: Elissa Rabellino   INDEX: Stimson Indexing
COVER/JACKET DESIGN: Wes Youssi/M.80 Design   COVER PHOTO: Reny Preussker
PRODUCTION SERVICE: Linda Jupiter Productions

Dedicated with love to my husband, Chris,
and our son, Wolfgang

Contents

Preface

I was 24 years old, pregnant, scared, and unsure about what to do. I went out on a limb and told someone whom I didn't know very well about my situation, only to discover a universal truth: we all have our own hidden stories.

It was the middle of summer and well past closing time in the downtown Berkeley bar where Polly Hancock and I worked together as bartenders. We were counting up the till and dividing our tips. When I didn't partake in our customary end-of-shift drink, I couldn't help but tell her why: "I'm not drinking because I'm pregnant. I'm not sure what I'm going to do yet." I don't know what I thought she'd say or how I hoped she'd help. I just needed to tell someone.

I'll never forget what happened. Without hesitation, she replied: "I've had an abortion." Before Polly, no one had ever told me that she'd had an abortion.

Everything changed in that instant. To this day, I remember how it felt. It was as if the sky had opened up, or a lightbulb had gone off, or every secret that existed in the world had finally been revealed to me. I saw beneath the surface of real life. Once I took the risk to open up, Polly opened up to me.

A couple of weeks after that late-night conversation with Polly at the bar, I had an abortion. Because I now talk openly about this experience, which you will read about in more detail in chapter 1, others feel comfortable sharing their stories with me. In the 15-plus years since my abortion, it would be impossible to count how many others I've heard about, into the thousands. Even though listening to and sharing about these experiences has become commonplace in my life, their presence still astounds me. The depth and nuances, the gray areas, and the unexpected twists and turns of each person's own journey exist in stark contrast to what are considered the known, simple, black-and-white terms of the abortion debate. The two spheres—the private conversations about real, lived, personal abortion experiences and the public political debate over the rights of women and fetuses—seem to have little in common with each other.

Abortion is a part of all our lives in one way or another. When one in three women will have an abortion in her lifetime,[1] there are few people the experience doesn't touch, whether it is a distant aunt who never emotionally recovered from her abortion; a brother who never talks about his high school girlfriend's abortion; or your own mother, whose illegal experience made her the fierce activist for abortion rights that she is today. Yet the debate seems so remote from these intimate family histories that even Barack Obama infamously remarked that he couldn't comment on the theological and scientific perspectives on the matter because it was "above [his] pay grade."[2]

The mistake is to think that the answer about what to do about abortion in this country will be resolved by religion, science, judicial process, or legislative policy. Facts and figures, logic, faith, values, and spirituality may inform our own personal and cultural beliefs, but in a diverse democracy like America, there is no one path, or one final answer, that can ultimately resolve the issue to everyone's liking. Accepting and acknowledging abortion for all its complexity can move our nation out of the abortion wars and toward peace.

Achieving this goal is simple, yet incredibly difficult. It demands a shift away from judgment and toward empathy, and it requires treating others as we would like to be treated. I must add: in the midst of a heated, passionate, high-stakes fight.

Go ahead and imagine how you would like to be treated as a fetus or as a woman who is pregnant and doesn't know what to do, but that is not what I am getting at. What I want is for you to think about how you would want to be treated when you found yourself in the throes of the most passionate and important argument of your lifetime.

Are you willing to treat your opponent with the same respect that you desire?

My guess is that being mocked and ridiculed or told you're stupid and wrong is not at the top of your list for how you would like to be treated in the midst of a fight. It's certainly not what I like, even from those who oppose me. Instead of seeing how much pain I can dish out to those I disagree with or who I believe have done me wrong, I seek to follow the golden rule and use my words and behavior to create more of what the world needs: love, compassion, and connection.

I want a future abortion conversation known for its openness, respect, and empathy, so instead of generating more heat, anger, and conflict, I practice *pro-voice*.

Pro-voice is a way of life. It is my religion. I have witnessed how the power of listening, storytelling, and embracing gray areas breaks through the rigid us-versus-them mentality that plagues enduring social conflicts such as abortion. Instead of being focused on attacking what's wrong, pro-voice focuses on highlighting and strengthening individual and social goods—such as our remarkable human capacity to love our enemies as ourselves—to generate new cultural norms.

• • •

"There isn't anyone you couldn't love once you've heard their story," Catholic pro-life, antiwar feminist peace crusader Mary Lou Kownacki once said.

Since Polly told me about her abortion, I've heard thousands of abortion stories of loss and regret, confidence and renewal, hope and tragedy, and trials and triumph. All along, I've also heard stories of infertility, miscarriage, adoption, and stillborn babies, though not nearly with the openness I experienced until I had my own story to reveal.

While writing this book, I got pregnant again. I was just a couple of weeks away from finishing my first full draft of this manuscript when I received some difficult news about the health of my baby that was discovered in a routine ultrasound. My husband and I, along with our families, went on an emotional roller coaster as we learned new information about what our baby, and thus our entire family, could expect to experience in the hours, days, weeks, and years after his birth. As I've talked openly with some of my friends about our situation, I've heard new stories about their own birth and parenting experiences—of what it was like to be adopted with their birth mom in prison, to adopt after multiple miscarriages, the experience of giving birth to one live baby while its twin was stillborn, stories of premature birth, and more—stories I might never have heard had I never opened up about my own struggles.

This is the type of storytelling that I call authentic. It's personal, intimate, and meaningful. It's as natural as breathing. Hearing stories, especially vulnerable, hard-to-talk-about ones, opens something within us, and we can't help but find a way to connect with the person revealing our own hidden truths. Often, we connect by sharing our own story.

There is a striking difference in the conversations that were available to me after my abortion and the ones that have happened since the birth of my son. Whereas talking openly about my complicated feelings after my abortion in the public sphere had made me into a political pariah because others feared how my story would impact the abortion wars, with my recent pregnancy, I had never been asked "How are you feeling?" so often in my life. And people seemed to want to know and care about the answer. There was no shortage of listening ears, and however I replied—whether I was feeling wonderful and excited or scared and unsure—there was always a "Been there!" response. I wasn't alone. There was no worry that any of my emotions about pending motherhood could have a political impact on the rights of other people to become parents.

The difficult birth and parenting stories I now hear aren't being told to me in order to get me to vote a certain way, or to indoctrinate me to an ideology or religion. Parents tell each other these stories because no matter how different our situations or outcomes, we're letting each other know that in some small way, we get it. We've been there, too. We're not alone. In their stories, what I understand is not that different from what I heard that night in Polly's admission: others have found themselves in unexpected situations too, have had to make difficult choices, have felt loss and sadness and yet, also, hope and love. Somehow they persevered, and they expect that I will, too. We all get through it. We all make our best life and establish our new normal. We are forever changed, and we move on.

These types of intimate conversations about abortion have been practically nonexistent in the public sphere, especially within the political one. But this is changing rapidly. More and more stories about abortion are finding their way out of the shadows and into the light, in entertainment such as the movie *Obvious Child* and television shows such as *Parenthood* and *Friday Night Lights*. However, it is the growing wave of public reveals by women who have had abortions that is leading the cultural change by disrupting the status quo with their personal stories. In the political realm, Jackie Speier (D-Calif.) was the first U.S. Representative to talk about her abortion on the floor of Congress. Speier's spontaneous confession in 2011 was soon followed by those of women leaders who made their abortion experience part of their political campaigns, such as Wendy Davis, a 2014 candidate for governor in Texas, and Lucy Flores, who talked openly about her abortion while running for lieutenant governor in Nevada in 2014. Taking matters into their own hands, such women as Angie Jackson, the first woman who live-tweeted her abortion, in 2010, and Emily Letts, the first woman who shared a video of her abortion on YouTube, in 2014, have pushed the envelope of self-expression online, opening the floodgates for more stories to be told.

A lot is at stake with this new openness about personal abortion experiences.

How we—as a society and a culture—handle it will impact not only the larger debate but also the women and families who experience abortion. I hope we use this rare cultural moment to do something greater than claim a winner or loser in the abortion wars. Let's give this outpouring the respect it deserves by taking a fresh look at how we can better support people who have abortions and peacefully address our political differences.

Pro-voice can help. Its tools of listening, storytelling, and embracing gray areas can became the predominant, expected cultural practice for talking about abortion.

Imagine what a difference this approach can make in the debate. It isn't a task just for lawmakers and judges. Infusing the cultural wars with love, respect, and empathy is the responsibility of everyone who cares about the health and wellbeing of women, our families and communities, and our democracy.

What are you willing to do to make that happen?

Throughout *Pro Voice*, I seek to show rather than tell what can happen when we let enemy thinking go and treat others respectfully—even when we are under threat and attack. If you get anything out of this book, I hope you will see the possibilities for entirely different conversations about abortion—and other social conflicts—in our country. We can have real heart-to-heart conversations generated out of our shared lived experiences with abortion and so many other hidden stories.

Introduction

My daughter has a lot of issues; she's into drugs and trouble," Angela (not her real name) said in Spanish. "When I was pregnant, I was scared and didn't know what to do, and I thought about having an abortion. I think God is punishing me just for thinking about it."

Angela was one of a dozen women sitting in a circle talking about how abortion had had an impact on their lives and the lives of their loved ones. The discussion was facilitated by my organization, Exhale, at a local job-training program for immigrant women in San Francisco. In addition to skills training in computers and electronics, the program connected the women to local community resources like ours. Exhale, the nonprofit organization that I cofounded after my own abortion and have been leading since 2000, offers a national, multilingual support talkline for women and men who need to talk about their abortion experiences—free of judgment and politics. Since our launch, thousands of people from around the world have called our confidential service to talk about their abortions.

Angela is not alone. Like her, many people who have never actually had an abortion feel strongly about it, and their views are shaped by their own personal, hidden stories.

Every reader of this book likely has two things in common with Angela. Whether or not you've personally experienced abortion, you probably have some kind of story that connects you—deeply and intimately—to the topic. And, as

1

with Angela, this personal relationship shapes your views and perspectives on the issue.

This is true for any issue mired in social conflict, whether it's racism, gun-violence prevention, or childhood vaccinations. The stories we tell and the stories we hear shape our collective perceptions and define our opinions and positions. Without making space for these personal stories to be heard, we can't get to the heart of the matter, which is why listening is at the root of what it means to be pro-voice.

My Exhale cofounders and I developed pro-voice because we wanted our talkline service to be available to all women who have had an abortion—women who felt regret and those who felt relief, women who are feminists and those who are not, pro-choice and pro-life women who have had an abortion, and everyone else—as well as the men and other loved ones who are a part of their lives. Yet, every time my cofounders and I talked about our vision and our plans to offer an emotional support service, the first question we always got—and often still do—was whether or not we were "for or against abortion." For an after-abortion service, being for or against abortion is beside the point. All of our callers already made their choice. Our job isn't to decide whether or not theirs was the right or wrong decision but to make sure that they get the unconditional love and support they need to move forward and have healthy lives.

The world needs pro-voice because what Exhale has been doing—listening without judgment—shouldn't be isolated to the realm of charity, a confidential talkline service, or even the subject of abortion. It must become the expected social behavior for how to address controversial issues when there are real human stories hidden behind the fight.

It may be hard to believe, but Exhale has worked specifically on abortion for more than 15 years, and we have never taken a political stand for or against its legality. And yet, we've had incredible and far-reaching social impact.

Exhale has led the way and initiated ideas for talking about personal abortion experiences that are increasingly accepted and mainstream across the political spectrum. When we started Exhale, we were chastised by abortion advocates for publicly acknowledging the gray areas of abortion experiences, but now organizations such as Planned Parenthood do it, too. Exhale's mission to create a stigma-free culture around abortion was initially criticized as weak by political activists, but now leaders like NARAL Pro-Choice America's Ilyse Hogue recognize the threat that stigma holds for women's equal rights. Magazines such as the *New Yorker, Glamour,* and *Cosmopolitan* let the voices of women who have had abortions stand on the merit of their own words, without outsider commentary. Most important, activists on all sides are now willing and able to articulate the fact that each woman's experience with abortion is unique and deserving of support and respect.

The culture is changing around abortion. It's time to leave the war mentality behind.

Born in the heart of nonviolence, pro-voice affirms the humanity of everyone involved in the fight. The antidote to polarizing, toxic dynamics, pro-voice replaces secrets with openness, dismantles stigma with support, overcomes judgment with respect, and establishes intimate connections where divides previously dominated.

The benefits of listening when the world wants a fight can be hard to measure—and yet, I have witnessed its positive impact many times.

On a clear November morning in 2009, I was sitting in the shiny new Southwest terminal in Oakland, California, watching my Twitter stream explode with reaction to the Stupak-Pitts Amendment. Stupak-Pitts, designed to prevent the Affordable Care Act from paying for abortions, got everyone I knew worked up. It was the fight of a lifetime for many activists who had spent their careers advocating on behalf of our nation's poor, the vulnerable victims of so many ideological policies.

I was headed to Los Angeles, where a longtime friend and donor to Exhale was hosting a fundraising house party on our behalf. One of the original founders of the California Black Women's Health Project, Fran Jemmott, was dedicated to talking about abortion in the lives of African American women.

On that morning I felt really torn. How could I raise money for women to have a place to talk about their abortions while I stayed silent on a big fight that would affect the lives of so many of them? Was Exhale's mission silly and soft, just like our critics said? Was this the time to stop listening and start fighting?

I was unsure about how to be a pro-voice leader in that moment, on that day.

A few hours later, I was sitting on Fran's couch in her living room with about 15 other women of all ages, from their early 20s to their late 70s. It was a diverse group of women of color, mostly African American. Fran kicked things off, welcoming her guests and talking about her history with Exhale. A former program officer at a large foundation in California, Fran had given Exhale one of our first significant grants. Then, unprompted and unplanned, she shared her abortion story. She asked the next woman to introduce herself to the group. The same thing happened. She shared her story, too. One by one, each woman spoke, introducing herself and then telling her abortion story.

Every woman in the room had at least one abortion story to share, and some had stories of birth and miscarriage to share, too. There were stories of legal and illegal abortions, of abortions necessitated by economic reasons or because of family violence or abuse. Other stories were about the importance of family pride and reputation, not wanting to let their family down by having a baby at a young age. Their stories were so different—their reasons, their reactions, and the way they told them, some in tears, others more matter-of-fact. The diversity of stories in the room was striking.

I had yet to say a single word. But by the time everyone had spoken, I knew why I was there and why I wasn't in Washington, DC, fighting about Stupak-Pitts. I knew why Exhale kept listening, even in the midst of fighting. I knew why our mission was powerful and important, because, without saying a word, something meaningful was able to emerge.

"Wouldn't it be amazing," I finally said, "if the way we talk about abortion in this country was done in just the way it happened here in this room? That's Exhale's mission.

"Today," I continued, "there is a big fight happening in Washington, DC, over abortion, and I am here with you because Exhale wants fewer fights and less judgment and more connecting like we're doing right now. What you all did naturally and without prompting is exactly what the future of abortion conversations needs to look like."

Later, Fran revealed to me what a big risk it had been for her high-profile friends to even attend such an event. Yet, their participation and willingness to share their intimate stories also revealed a deeper sense of trust and connection. "The need to bear witness," Fran affirmed, "is a revered cultural and community tradition."

That day wasn't the only time I had doubts about the power of pro-voice to make a difference. I have plenty of moments of uncertainty. But each time I consider joining the fight, I remember that fighting only leads to more fighting. If I want more listening in the world, the best way to make that happen is to keep listening and to inspire others to listen more, too.

Anyone can be pro-voice. Open source, pro-voice is a set of tools and techniques that are freely available to those who share a commitment to overcome debilitating conflicts by finding the connections among the divides, and by being empathetic and respectful instead of judgmental. Republicans and Democrats, pro-choice and pro-life advocates, religious people and atheists—all can be pro-voice if they are willing to listen and share personally with the goal of transforming social conflict from war into peace.

My goal is that readers of *Pro-Voice* will find inspiration, ideas, direction, and hope that will help them to apply pro-voice in their own lives and to navigate the conflicted issues they care about most.

Chapter 1

The Birth of Pro-Voice

I grew up in the middle of our nation's wars over abortion.

In 1976, the year I was born, the first clinic bombing was reported. The 1980s, my formative childhood years, were dominated by the impact of aggressive pro-life protests. California, my home state, had one of the most successful anti-abortion campaigning organizations around: more than 40,000 pro-life activists were arrested while protesting abortion clinics during a four-year period in the '80s.[1]

As I was growing up in Southern California, it wasn't unusual for me to see a huge picture of a bloody, dismembered fetus on a massive sign attached to the side of a minivan driving up and down the freeways near my home. I was certainly affected by pro-life public-awareness efforts but unaware of the violence against clinics. I grew up without a TV, so if these events were covered on the news, I never saw them.

As regular attendees of what I like to call a "surfing Christian" church and school, both nondenominational, my family and I spent time with other church and school families on the beaches of my hometown. San Clemente is steeped in surfing culture: it's the home of *Surfing Magazine*; surf legends such as the Paskowitz, Fletcher, Beschen, and Gudauskas families; iconic surf brands such as Rainbow Sandals and Astrodeck; the nonprofit ocean conservation organization the Surfrider Foundation.[2] To top it all off, our "Spanish Village by the Sea" was made famous by Richard Nixon during his presidency as the location of his "western White House." Everyone, including many of the moms and all the kids, surfed, and in our circle, a special occasion meant it was time to pull out a nice Hawaiian shirt or sundress and wear the good flip-flops. Only the preacher wore a suit. Everyone was pro-life, and we all mourned the tragedy of abortion, but no one ever invited me to a protest, and as far as I knew, no one in our community participated in one, either—violent or not.

But we did put our pro-life Christian views into practice. Ever since I was young, my family and I traveled with church groups to Tijuana on missionary trips where I never saw anyone preach or try to convert others. We were there to chip in and help local orphanages survive. The dads worked on building clean bathrooms, and the moms spent all day in the kitchen making food. My younger sister and I spent the day hanging out with the babies. As a young girl, I found it hard to hear that the baby sitting on my lap—the one resigned to the flies in her eyes, nose, and mouth, despite my constant attempts to shoo them away—had been found by one of the adults at the local trash dump, where they went early each morning to look for abandoned babies. I loved babies. In fact, I spent less time with my own peers in Sunday school class than in the nursery, caring for the infants during church services.

Outside of these trips to Tijuana, it wasn't unusual for my dad to bring home a stranger he had just met who needed a place to crash for the night, or for my family to spend Thanksgiving at a local soup kitchen. We lived pretty close to the bone ourselves. My parents basically made minimum wage in the 1980s, and I never earned an allowance. I started making my own money at 10 years old with—you guessed it— babysitting gigs, and the money I started to save then helped me pay for college later. But that wasn't my only job. I also had a paper route at 10, the first girl to get the job from the local boys. Even though I read the paper every day before making my rounds, I don't remember tracking the abortion fights.

Our community was white, working class, and not well educated—the dads I knew were plumbers, contractors, and teachers, and most of the moms worked as assistants and receptionists in local doctors' offices or were teachers too. When I was young, my dad had every kind of odd job—bee-keeper, chimney sweep—and my mom worked as a cocktail waitress. My dad would often take my little sister and me to have hot cocoa at the bar when my mom was working late into the night. Later on, both of my parents got better jobs working for the wealthy—my dad as a private pilot for company CEOs and my mom as a housecleaner. Homeschooled for a few years, I often did my work at the kitchen tables of families whose homes were several times the size of our own while my mom scrubbed their houses clean.

We all cared about God, the less fortunate, and the ocean. I don't remember a single political conversation, but I do know that I was raised with a charitable bent in our pro-life views, not a violent, judgmental one. As a kid, I remember a couple of teenage girls who got pregnant and had babies at a young age, and I promised myself that it would never happen to me. It was hard to believe that I could ever be in that position, getting pregnant when I didn't want to be. If the unlikely ever happened, I always assumed I'd have the baby.

I knew I could never kill my baby if I got pregnant. And then I did.

• • •

I had come a long way since my childhood on the beaches of San Clemente. I'd followed in the family footsteps set out by my grandfather, my uncle, and my dad, who had all worked as professional pilots, and started taking flying lessons while still in high school. I was learning how to land a single-engine Cessna airplane at small airports throughout San Diego while I got to know the Alaskan bush-pilot character of Maggie O'Connell on *Northern Exposure* along with the rest of America. After graduation, I quickly made my way to Alaska, where I learned how to land a plane on rivers, lakes, and glaciers, among having other adventures.

They say that women headed to Alaska alone are either running to or running from a man, and upon arrival they find that the "odds may be good" for finding a husband but the "goods are odd." The Fairview Inn in Talkeetna, where I lived for a summer working for a local bush-flying outfit, had photo albums full of local men looking for a female mate. Their main requirements for a potential partner were that the woman be "quiet" and be able to "skin a moose." Beyond its breathtaking beauty, the quirky honesty of Alaska was one of the things I loved the most.

There's a lot of freedom in such a big place, and with it comes the harsh realities of inhabiting a rugged, wild land. Getting charged by a mama grizzly bear on a deserted trail once was enough for me. So too was knowing that not all of the courageous, passionate mountaineers I met would come back from their adventures alive. When I was 20 years old,

I hauled the body bag of an older East German man off a small plane and had to organize how to get his remains and belongings home. Before he headed into the mountains, I'd spent hours with him and his climbing partner, who talked about how they dreamed of climbing Denali while confined by communism behind the Berlin Wall. The man's dream ended tragically in an avalanche, and yet he inspired me to always pursue my own.

After Alaska and a brief stop living at home, attending community college in Orange County, I got accepted into UC Berkeley. I paid my way through school, selling everything from lattes and cocktails to bikes and skis at the local REI while earning my degree in peace and conflict studies. A voracious reader who had spent hours at the local library from a young age, I discovered and was politically transformed by *The Autobiography of Malcolm X* at age 15. By reading his story, I learned how to connect the dots between the hardships I saw in Tijuana or at the local soup kitchen and a broader social system of inequality and discrimination. I sought a college education that would teach me how to right the wrongs of injustice. I imagined that after graduation, I'd travel the globe on peaceful, humanitarian missions to serve those hurt in conflict zones and uplift those silenced by political repression.

Then everything changed—sort of. Three months after graduating college and three months into a new relationship, I found out that I was pregnant.

I thought I'd have the baby, until I told the guy. He wanted me to get an abortion. It forced me to take the option seriously in a way I never had before. It was hard to come up with a picture of what an abortion would mean in my life.

I could see the dismembered fetus on the side of the mini-
vans from my childhood, yet I had no corresponding image
of a woman who'd had one. No one had ever told me she'd
had an abortion. I could only remember one rumor years
before about a girl from high school whom I hadn't known
well, but everyone else I knew had had their babies. I had no
idea how to make the decision. What criteria should I use?
How would I know what the right decision was? Would I
regret an abortion later?

It was during this time that I took the risk to confide in
my friend Polly while we were closing up the downtown
Berkeley bar where we both worked. When she told me
about her own abortion, Polly gave me an unusual gift: the
knowledge that I was not alone in my experience. Whatever I decided, someone I knew had been through this, too.

It was the strangest feeling to walk around pregnant, not
wanting to be, knowing that I had this big secret and that
no one could tell just by looking at me. I found myself more
curious about other people's private lives. What secrets were
people holding that I couldn't see? What major life decisions
were they facing? Whom could they talk to?

The old adage about walking a mile in someone else's
shoes came alive. I promised myself that I would never judge
anyone again. I hadn't lived their life. I didn't know what
they knew, fear what they feared, hope what they hoped. I
knew that we all needed the same thing: not to be rescued
or saved from the pain and difficulty of our circumstances
and choices, but to feel cared for and supported as we fought
our own battles.

In the end, having the abortion was not so much about
staying on some kind of life track or "getting back to normal"

as it was about my need to sever all ties I had with the guy. It
was a step toward the unknown. The abortion forced me to
let go of the future I had spent several days imagining after
I found out that I was pregnant. I wasn't going to be a mom
this time. I said goodbye to all the ideas, strategies, plans,
and hopes I'd come up with as I tried to make having a baby
work out somehow in my life. There is no do-over with abortion. I could never take it back. I knew it would always hold
a place in my life's story, and with just a few days to make
such a life-altering decision, I had no way to know if it was
the best one for me.

I didn't know who I would be after an abortion.

While I had been aware of the abortion debate before
my abortion, I didn't give it much attention. After my abortion, I listened more carefully, but all I heard was yelling
and screaming. Noise. Anger. Outrage. It seemed to come
from all sides. I couldn't distinguish one side's voice from
the other. It was toxic and polarizing and full of judgment,
finger-pointing, and blame. I felt grateful for my legal, cov-
ered-by-health-insurance abortion—absolutely—and yet once
it was over, I was pretty mixed up about it.

I didn't hear a voice like mine in the debate.

I searched for support, people and places to go talk to
about my abortion. Even in Berkeley, California, all I found
were Christian, pro-life organizations that wanted me to
seek forgiveness from God. That wasn't what I needed. The
pro-choice side had nothing to offer. If the pro-life side
considered abortion one of life's biggest sins, then the pro-
choice side seemed to consider it no big deal, an experience not worth talking about. I eventually found my way to
a private therapist whom I paid in the cash I earned from

my bartending tips. Ever since I'd known what an abortion was, I told myself I'd never have one, and then I did.
I didn't know if my abortion was aligned with my values or
an aberration, inconsistent with who I was. My life wasn't
so black and white anymore. It had gotten very, very gray.

I now knew that I wasn't alone, but I didn't understand
why people weren't talking about their own abortions. I wondered how things would change if we did.

I no longer needed to travel the globe to support and
uplift those hurt by conflict and repression. America's abortion wars were in desperate need of their own humanitarian, peaceful mission, and I was determined to respond to
the crisis.

Nonviolence Reimagined

In his final book, *Where Do We Go From Here: Chaos or Community?* Dr. Martin Luther King Jr. wrote, "I suggest that the
philosophy and strategy of nonviolence become immediately
a subject for study and for serious experimentation in every
field of human conflict."[3]

After my abortion, I took up Dr. King's challenge. I wanted
to put my peaceful values into action and experiment with
nonviolence on the issue that had unexpectedly landed at
my front door. I now had a personal stake in the abortion
debate, but I didn't want to fight to win. I wanted to transform the war into peace.

Since 2000, I have devoted my life to this experiment.

I cofounded Exhale to put nonviolent theories and ideas
into real-life practice. Our programs and messages infuse
love, compassion, and connection into the polarizing debate,

diffusing tensions, increasing understanding, and promoting wellbeing. Listening and storytelling are the primary tools of our trade. The gray area is our landscape. We coined "pro-voice" in 2005 to inspire others to join our growing movement of peacemakers.

Months after my abortion, as I was researching abortion on the way to founding Exhale, I walked into a local Berkeley bookstore in search of a self-help book for women who'd had abortions. I was hoping to find something that could provide detailed information about all aspects of the procedure—from the medical and physical elements to the emotional ones—with voices of women sharing their stories and advice, including the ways they felt about the loss of their fetus. I found nothing like it on the shelves, so I went to the clerk to ask for help.

When I told her my request, she looked nervously at me, turned red, got flustered, and blurted out, "But abortion is a choice!" She may have repeated it a few times.

"True," I said, "and I was hoping to find a book about women's experiences."

"All abortion books are under politics," she said before walking away quickly.

I looked under politics, and sure enough, there were a few books about abortion there, but nothing was written for a woman who'd had one or was thinking

about having one. Abortion was considered a political, private choice, but rarely was it addressed in
personal terms. The clerk at the Berkeley bookstore
wasn't the only one to think of abortion so narrowly.

As much as I liked and appreciated the doctor who
did my abortion, he gave me the same message.
He made it a point to say that I'd never have to tell
another person about it. He informed me that no
doctor would be able to tell that I'd ever had one.
From the very beginning, the message was that my
abortion was private, a secret, not something to be
shared with others, even my other doctors.

Later, a fertility specialist told me at a conference how much this sentiment had hurt his practice, because women later in life who were trying to
get pregnant would hide their past abortions out of
shame. But, he told me, a past pregnancy is one of
the best indicators of someone's future ability to get
pregnant. A patient's hiding of such critical information made it difficult for the doctor to understand his
patient's whole history, and it prevented him from
offering real, medically proven hope to the woman
and her partner.

We at Exhale weren't alone in our desire to forge a new
way forward on the abortion debate. The year we adopted
"pro-voice," Asian Communities for Reproductive Justice
(now called Forward Together) published their vision for a
broad-based reproductive justice movement led by women

of color, and pro-choice leader Frances Kissling published her seminal piece "Is There Life After Roe?" on the importance of valuing the fetus alongside women's rights.[4] Anna Quindlen wrote in *Newsweek* that in all her years as an opinion columnist, the debate over abortion had hardly changed, noting, "Leaders of the opposing sides have been frozen into polar positions." Quindlen acknowledged that abortion doesn't fit "neatly into black-and-white boxes, it takes place in that messy gray zone of hard choices," writing that "we insult ourselves by leaving its complexities unexamined."[5]

During his 2009 commencement address at Notre Dame, President Obama put out a call for more civility, asking opposing sides to at least try to "discover the possibility of finding common ground" and help "transform the culture war into a tradition of cooperation and understanding."[6] But when the next abortion battle was waged a year later, this time over the Stupak-Pitts Amendment, which would limit abortion funding in the Affordable Care Act, the common-ground rhetoric was quickly abandoned in favor of the usual polarizing talking points.

There is a better way to do this, but the conflict is so effective at sweeping the nation into its vicious cycles that resistance to its power is short-lived.

There have been a handful of efforts designed to confront America's abortion wars over the last 40 years. The most famous attempt is the one led by the nonpartisan Public Conversations Project, in response to the 1994 murder of two women who worked in a Brookline, Massachusetts, abortion-providing clinic. For five years, six pro-life and pro-choice leaders met in facilitated confidential conversations in an attempt to practice mutual respect across their differences.

After Dr. George Tiller, one of just a few doctors who per-
formed abortions later in pregnancy, was murdered in his
church in Wichita, Kansas, in 2009, the pro-choice website
RH Reality Check (rhrealitycheck.org) launched an online
effort called "Common Ground" with the hope of bridging
America's divide on abortion. But the forum lacked the full
support of RH Reality Check's leadership, and so it lasted
less than a year.

In all cases, the focus of these peace initiatives has been
on the activists and the leaders actively engaged on both
sides of the fight. Not a single common-ground effort has
sought to include or directly address the lived experiences
of people with abortion. Exhale is the first to attempt to put
the voices and leadership of women—and men—who have
gone through abortions at the center of organizing efforts
for abortion conflict transformation.

Exhale's pro-voice philosophy is a 15-year experiment in
the application of nonviolence to America's cultural conflict
over abortion. We didn't invent pro-voice to help one side
or the other of the abortion wars to declare a final victory,
nor was it created with any particular set of policy goals or
objectives in mind, even those considered "common ground."
Pro-voice is an evolving theoretical framework with a set of
concrete tools to help people and groups create meaningful
connections across their differences—whether they are political, personal, or cultural—with the goal of making conflict
more compassionate and respectful. It has applications and
benefits far beyond the issue of abortion.

Pro-Voice = Listening + Storytelling

At one end of the room was a sign that said "Agree." The other end had a sign that said "Disagree." Standing at different points across the spectrum in between were women of different ages and ethnicities. One was visibly pregnant. They had just heard the statement "Abortion is a form of killing" and had moved to stand in the position that indicated their vote. "It's not a baby yet," said one young woman standing under Disagree, "so I don't think it's killing." "Everything in your body is alive, so just like you kill cancer living in your body, an abortion kills something that is living," said another, who was standing under Agree, adding, "I don't know if it matters whether or not it's a baby."

Hearing this exchange, other women in the group changed their positions. They moved to different areas on the spectrum and then shared their reasons why. More statements, such as "It's better to have an abortion early in pregnancy" and "Abortion is a form of birth control," were read out loud by the trainer. Each time, the women moved to different points across the spectrum between Agree and Disagree, and each time, they spoke about where they had landed and why.

Often, people shifted their positions after listening to others speak.

The 12 women going through the exercise were all in training to be talkline counselors at Exhale. Each of them had applied and then been carefully screened and interviewed before being accepted into a 60-hour training, in which they learned how to answer calls from women and men in search of emotional support after an abortion. As a group,

these women explored such questions as whether abortion
was killing, because many of the people they would be talking to on the phone had considered it that way.

The goal of this training exercise was not to find agreement among the group or even to debate the statements.
Instead, the exercise was used to surface how diverse values
and beliefs can shape our understanding of personal abortion experiences, even among a like-minded group of people who share a common goal.

The trainer had done this exercise with volunteers many
times, and when she closed it, she always asked the group,
"Can you imagine doing this exercise with people we gather
randomly off the street outside our office? Talking about
abortion in this way is not safe in public or with strangers,
which is why it's so important that we create a safe space
for women and men to feel heard, no matter what, on our
talkline."

Ten years later, in the middle of winter in New York
City, three young women stood in front of a room of complete strangers, a classroom of college students, and shared
their layered, complicated personal truths about abortion.
Not a single one of their stories fit easily into a box marked
pro-choice or pro-life. In fact, one of them told how it was
these very boxes that had caused her so much distress after
her abortion. She couldn't make her feelings fit a political
agenda. In any typical public setting, these women's stories
would raise the question "What's the point?" Stories about
abortion are usually told in simple, black-and-white terms
with clear moral and political agendas.

However, these stories were ambiguous, and yet their
impact was undeniable.

"This workshop isn't what I expected," one student said. "I came in wearing my armor. It turns out I didn't need it."

Exhale's 2013 national Sharing Our Stories Tour—a program in which five women shared their personal abortion stories with people on college campuses, in churches, and in community centers across the country—shattered expectations and dismantled stale assumptions about what happens when abortion is discussed openly between people who have different views on the topic. In Austin, Milwaukee, Chicago, New York City, and the San Francisco Bay Area, the women shared their stories in pro-voice workshops they led, teaching audiences how to be empathetic through listening and storytelling.

Heavily evaluated by a consulting firm specializing in measuring social impact, audiences reported that they had been moved and transformed by what they had experienced.[7] Here are some of the comments that the audiences shared:

- "Due to the diversity of perspectives and feelings, I felt . . . more willing to share my experience and ask questions."

- "I was surprised by the speakers' compassion, empathy, and sensitivity to those who oppose them."

- "I am personally pro-life and often feel shut out or judged because of my opinion. However, I could one day be in the same position and respect everyone regardless of political stance."

- "It made me feel at ease to learn that men have a role and a place in all of this that is respected and appreciated."

- ◆ "In the future, I will be more thoughtful about when it's appropriate to engage politically and when it's better just to hear a person as a human being."

Over 88 percent of audiences on the tour heard a new perspective about women's experiences with abortion. And the diversity of the abortion stories helped create an environment where different feelings, thoughts, and opinions were welcome. Ninety-seven percent of audience members thought that the workshop was respectful of diverse experiences.

These pro-voice workshops broke every rule about what's supposed to happen when strangers talk openly about abortion. You can do it, too. With pro-voice as your guide, controversial topics like abortion can bring people together, not drive them apart.

In *Pro-Voice*, I show how listening, storytelling, and embracing gray areas create unexpected possibilities. I offer stories, case studies, and ideas that I hope will inspire readers to make pro-voice their own. For the purposes of this book, I focus on the high-level principles and components that are fundamental to the pro-voice practice. I review how America got so stuck on abortion and the challenges that women who have abortions face when they speak personally and publicly about their lives. I explore what it takes to infuse creativity and openness into a decades-long stalemate; and I share the successes, failures, and lessons learned in the pro-voice experiment thus far.

Throughout this book, I use the phrases "women who have had abortions," "people who experience abortion," and "women and men" in an attempt to acknowledge the incredibly diverse array of people who are directly affected by an abortion. There are many challenges in speaking to and about all these groups, including the limitation of pronouns to represent the spectrum of gender identities and the natural emphasis on the lived experience of a person who physically undergoes the abortion procedure. Remember that even a secret abortion still takes place within the context of a woman's relationships, however healthy or abusive they may be. Her partner, family, and friends have their own personal experiences of her abortion, as do those providing her medical care. Though I use the term *fetus* throughout the book, I am quite comfortable calling it a *baby* or an *unborn child*. No word is off-limits if it's been used by a woman to describe her own experience with abortion, and no political alignment is implied in my own word choice.

These are the guiding beliefs of the pro-voice philosophy:

Pro-voice connections are radical acts of courage that can change the world. In the midst of hostility, attacks, and demonization, creating meaningful connections across differences generates new possibilities for change and transformation.

Embracing a diversity of voices, including those that are hidden, reveals new possibilities. Whether it's the pro-choice woman who regrets her abortion, the pro-life woman relieved by hers, or the experiences of the men involved in abortion decisions, the voices and stories that disrupt conventional black-and-white thinking create opportunities for new ideas to emerge.

Separation damages human dignity. Not only must we advocate respect for our own humanity, but also we must affirm and sustain the dignity of our opponents.

Personal experiences should shape political reality. People's real, lived experiences with polarized issues or stigmatized experiences can humanize toxic dynamics and illustrate complexity hidden within us-versus-them perceptions.

We continue the work of a long and powerful line of peacemakers. We have been influenced and inspired by those who have chosen love over hate and accept the task to do the same with the modern challenges of our evolving society.

All pro-voice strategies should be designed with the following goals:

- Rehumanize toxic dynamics
- Affirm and sustain human dignity
- Generate creativity and imagination
- Spur innovative thinking and action
- Invite openness, engagement, and conversation where before there was black-and-white or us-versus-them thinking

Pro-voice tools have been piloted, tested, experimented with, fixed, adapted, improved, and perfected in a wide range of forums, online and in person, in big groups and small, with people of diverse values, beliefs, backgrounds, and experiences around the country. Each tool can be broken down into any number of specific steps to form a curriculum tailored for a range of individual, community, and organizational purposes.

These are the core tools of the pro-voice philosophy:

Listening. Central to Exhale's work from the very beginning, active listening to truly understand where a person is coming from is the cornerstone of pro-voice practice.

Storytelling. It's essential to let go of the desire to make the most persuasive narrative and instead support people as they tell their own stories, in their own words, and in their own time.

Embrace gray areas. The creativity and innovations needed for cultural change come from the ability to accept the ambiguities of human experiences.

Exhale's community has been inspired and galvanized by what takes place in the intimate moments of connection between a talkline caller and an Exhale counselor, between women who are sharing abortion stories with each other, and between a storyteller and her audience. Given that there are often great differences between a storyteller and her audience, a counselor and a caller, or two women swapping stories with one another—they may be of different races, ethnicities, religions, ages, or education levels; they may speak with different accents and wear different styles; and they may have vastly different opinions about abortion—they can still connect in ways that empower, inspire, and make them hopeful for the future. These moments exist because even though the subject matter is highly polarizing, a pro-voice person will offer compassion and respond with empathy instead of defensiveness, even when under threat.

Practicing pro-voice behavior makes one incredibly vulnerable.

This type of nonviolent response—responding to hate with love or to attack with pacifism—has been called "moral jiu-jitsu."[8] By flipping the script, by changing expectations about how one is supposed to respond to hostility, conflict, or distress, we disrupt us-versus-them thinking. Opponents are unsettled. Gandhi called this nonviolent response to oppression *satyagraha*, and Dr. King called it "soul force." One pro-choice activist referred to her work to publicly embrace the gray areas of abortion as a way to "take the wind out of the sails" of her pro-life enemies.

Pro-voice is the framework that applies these revolutionary concepts to the modern cultural warfare over abortion in America. Let's see the opportunities in the obstacles of the abortion conflict and listen to the real human stories hidden behind the fight.

Chapter 2

America's Abortion Conflict

Our country has never really talked about the personal experience of abortion.

For a long time, abortion was an open secret—illegal yet something everyone knew existed even though it was never discussed. When legal cases started making the news in the 1960s, the topic of abortion came out of the closet. But it wasn't the voices and experiences of women who were having abortions that were making the front page. It was most often stories about providers and local efforts to crack down on the procedure.

After LaVange Michael, a 68-year-old widow, was arrested for providing women with illegal abortions in her home in Rapid City, South Dakota, in 1962, the *New York Times* noted that it was no longer so easy to sweep abortion under the rug of secrecy.[1]

People were starting to talk openly about abortion and how it might be addressed.

It was the perfect time to make a change.

Social movements advocating for increased equality and the elimination of racism and sexism were sweeping across America, generating a heightened sense of urgency and new hope for the possibilities of a less restrictive and freer society. The arrest of Michael was just three years after "Bloody

27

Sunday," when hundreds of African Americans marching
from Selma to Montgomery, Alabama, for voting rights were
injured and tear-gassed, which prompted President Lyndon
B. Johnson to create the Voting Rights Act of 1965. It was
just a couple of years after 24-year-old Stokely Carmichael
was identified by the *New York Times* as the new chairman
of the Black Panther party,[2] signifying the growth, diversity, and splintering of black leadership in the movements
for civil rights and black power. The National Organization
for Women (NOW), cofounded by Betty Friedan, had just
called for equal partnership between the sexes, while Dolores
Huerta and César Chávez were forming the National Farm
Worker's Association, later called the United Farm Workers.

Everywhere, it seemed that people—especially women and
people of color—were fighting back in every way they knew
how: through nonviolent direct action, with violence, using
rhetoric and oratory, through consciousness-raising, writing,
publishing, protesting, and talking openly about the truth
of their hidden lives. The mood was infectious. The time to
make change—dramatic, drastic, far-reaching, and revolutionary change—was *now*.

One activist spoke about why fighting for abortion rights
was so important to her: "Part of it was just breaking out . .
. because everyone was feeling so repressed."[3]

America was changing rapidly. Those in favor of repeal-
ing the laws that banned abortion in every state felt hopeful that change was right around the corner. Robert McCoy,
coordinator of the Minnesota Council for the Legal Termi-
nation of Pregnancy, told the *New York Times* in 1968, "It is
really remarkable how much the climate for public opinion

had changed in just a few years . . . I wouldn't be surprised if several states including Minnesota soon repealed their abortion laws."[4] The movement for abortion rights had begun.

The 1960s Movement for Abortion Repeal

Abortion hadn't always been illegal in the United States. Historical records show a complicated legal picture dating back over a hundred years. Laws restricting abortion increased right alongside demand for it, creating a complicated social and legal web of repression and acceptance, availability and restriction. But the feminist activists of the '60s were done with keeping abortion behind closed doors. Situations like Michael's, where she had been operating safely out of her South Dakota home as an open secret for more than three decades, were no longer enough. It was time to make bigger demands.

Helping women to find safe providers was a key organizing strategy of the early grassroots movement to repeal the abortion laws. Most of the activists worked in clinics, Planned Parenthood offices, and other family-planning organizations as staff and volunteers or were young women who had been politicized by their experiences helping their friends get abortions. In her book *The Pro-Choice Movement: Organization and Activism in the Abortion Conflict*, Suzanne Staggenborg noted that most of the people who organized for repeal were "conscious constituents,"[5] people who became activists because they thought repeal was the right thing to do, not because they were expecting to personally benefit. Often, participation in the referral networks was what kept

activists motivated to keep working for change against the
odds. One woman said that helping connect women to abortion services was "a tonic; we couldn't have kept going in
New York without the constant reminders of women who
needed help."[6]

Patricia Maginnis, widely recognized as one of the first
abortion activists and founder of the Society for Humane
Abortion (SHA), had experienced an illegal abortion herself.
She often stood near the Mexican border on the other side
from Tijuana handing out leaflets about where to get safe
abortions, waiting to be arrested. She often was. Maginnis
developed an underground referral network that sent more
than 12,000 women outside the United States for abortions.[7]
Abortion referral was also the impetus for the formation
of Chicago's legendary "Jane" underground abortion collective. Its founder, Heather Booth, a white activist who had
participated in sit-ins to protest segregation and registered
black voters during Freedom Summer in Mississippi, was
moved to abortion activism after she helped a friend's pregnant sister get an abortion. She found herself helping more
and more women to find an abortion. Her abortion referral
network in Chicago—made infamous because its volunteer
members learned how to perform abortions themselves—
provided more than 11,000 abortions.[8]

It's clear that some of the early organizers, like Maginnis,
had personally experienced abortion, and that direct contact
with women who needed abortions, as Booth experienced,
was a great motivator for people to get involved in the movement. What remains unclear in the documented histories of
the abortion repeal and pro-choice movements is the role of
the women who were getting the abortions.

Some famous feminist activists, such as Gloria Steinem, were open about their abortions, and many less famous ones participated in public speak-outs, talking openly about their experiences, but what happened to the thousands of women who got illegal abortions through the referral networks? What was their ongoing function in the repeal efforts? Were the repeal activists actually the same women who were having abortions, like Maginnis, and if so, why weren't their experiences more publicly visible at the forefront of the movement? Or were the repeal activists and the abortion patients very different groups of women—one group needing help, the other group providing that help?

Certainly, there were plenty of barriers for women having abortions to speak openly and be the public face of their own movement; severe social rejection and fear of a range of repercussions, including investigation and prosecution, were very real. Yet, given how many activists were risking their lives for so many civil rights issues of the time, these aren't adequate reasons to explain their lack of visible participation—or the lack of documentation of it—during a time when social movements were sweeping the country, demonstrating the great lengths and major risks that people were willing to take to promote their own rights. Abused women risked their own lives to share their secrets with each other, becoming the leaders of their own movement to end domestic and sexual violence. The civil rights organizers of the South often spent years in hushed conversations with rural, uneducated black families, putting their own lives and the lives of the locals at risk in hopes of inspiring them to participate in the nonviolent actions that eventually brought down Jim Crow and changed the direction of our country forever.

Why didn't the public hear directly from women having illegal abortions?

Given the times, perhaps abortion repeal seemed a small and easy feat. Maybe activists thought that the change could happen quickly, given the mood of the country and its shifting social norms. Or perhaps it was a strategic choice: let's dispatch a few people to fix the nuisance of the illegality problem, but let's not waste precious time dismantling the cultural customs that instruct women to keep their abortions secret.

Maybe activists didn't see the private nature of abortion as a problem, only that it was illegal. Maybe they could never imagine that one day an abortion experience might be something that women *and men* would need to talk about openly—either with each other or publicly—so they never considered the benefits of helping to open the floodgates.

I can't help but wonder how the course of abortion reform—and thus the future of the abortion conversation in this country—might have been different if the people who had been leading the way were also the public face of personal abortion experiences.

Population Fears and Elitist Strategies for the Win

Liberal social movements didn't generate the only ideas influencing the mood and political landscape of the '60s. New fears about environmental degradation caused by the population explosion also grew, leading many activists and leaders to seek dramatic and far-reaching solutions to head off the impending crisis. According to the authors of *Undivided Rights: Women of Color Organize for Reproductive Justice*, these fears often led to abusive targeting of the fertility and repro-ductive choices of women of color.[9]

The movement to reduce the worldwide population encouraged federal government funding for family-planning efforts. Many feminists and women's health activists, includ-ing African American leaders, considered this a win, but it was greeted skeptically by some members of the African American community, who wondered if they were subjects of racist fertility control.[10] President Nixon gained support for family-planning efforts in 1970 by "appealing to whites' fears about population explosions." His advisers put together sta-tistics to show how the African American population would grow in the years ahead, warning of the potential for future social turbulence and leading white politicians to want to "help racial minorities limit their fertility." All of a sudden, pro-segregation southern politicians were ready to support family planning.[11]

It wasn't just concerns for the environment and the potential of social turbulence that sparked interest in pop-ulation-control efforts. Commercial and U.S. security con-cerns became linked to women of color reproducing. R. T. Ravenholt from USAID introduced a plan to sterilize a quar-ter of the world's women because, as he put it, "[p]opula-tion control is necessary to maintain the normal operations of US commercial interests around the world."[12]

While white women fought for the choice to *not* have children and demanded increased access to birth control and abortion, women of color were often fighting for the right to *have* their own children and for freedom from coer-cive policies designed to restrict their reproduction. Unfor-tunately, the different histories, experiences, and goals of

women who shared a desire for greater reproductive freedom and decision making have often clashed. According to
activist Angela Davis, these differences have created "disas-
trous political results . . . [which have] limited the reproductive rights of women of color and poor women."[13]

Dr. Judith Blake, the founding chair of demography at UC
Berkeley, was caught up in the population movement and
critical of the women's movement, which she believed cared
too much about supporting moms and families, an obstacle
to the population-control methods she favored. She set out to
better understand the public's views on abortion in the '60s,
concluding that the biggest resistance to abortion came from
poor and uneducated women. Therefore, Blake surmised in
1971, "changes in abortion laws, like most social changes, will
not come about by agitation at the grassroots level, or by the
activity of righteously indignant individuals who cannot cir-
cumvent existing statutes. Rather, it is to the educated and
the influential that we must look for effecting rapid legislative change in spite of conservative opinions among important subgroups such as the lower classes and women."[14]

In *The Pro-Choice Movement*, by Suzanne Staggenborg,
Lawrence Lader, a board member of the Association for
the Study of Abortion and later a cofounder and the chairman of NARAL, described why the early efforts at abortion
repeal focused on legislative lobbying and litigation rather
than popular referendums: "We weren't sure we could win
them, number one, and number two, we felt what was right
constitutionally and morally should not be voted on. I mean,
it sounds kind of undemocratic, but we felt it was right constitutionally and morally. If you took a vote on slavery, the
abolitionists might have lost."[15]

Another well-known activist, Lucinda Cisler, also believed that if abortion were left up to voters, they would vote against it. She was against efforts aimed at reforming current laws, insisting, like Lader, that anything less than women having complete control of their own decisions was an injustice.[16] The idea to reform the abortion laws over time through grassroots advocacy and organizing was abandoned in favor of going quickly after a more drastic goal: complete repeal of all abortion laws.

It was a political moment ripe for change, and yet neither the population activists nor the abortion-repeal activists had much faith in their ability to organize and generate widespread grassroots support for changing the legal landscape of abortion. Their chosen strategies—legislative lobbying and litigation—were, according to Staggenborg, "out of step with the pattern of protest in the decade in which the movement took shape."[17]

Two years after Blake's advocacy for an elitist solution to the abortion problem, a 27-year-old lawyer named Sarah Weddington, from Austin, Texas—a woman who had traveled to Mexico to have an illegal abortion in 1967—became the youngest person ever to successfully argue a Supreme Court case. The court's ruling on *Roe v. Wade* declared abortion a private right and dramatically changed the legal landscape of abortion throughout the United States.

It was January 22, 1973.

The issue went all the way to the Supreme Court because elite institutions such as the American College of Obstetricians and Gynecologists (ACOG), the American Medical Association (AMA), and the American Psychiatric Association had joined with the abortion reform advocates to push it to the top of the judicial system. When the court looked at the membership numbers of these and other groups that had signed on, such as NOW, which claimed 20,000 members in California, and Zero Population Growth, which had 300,000 nationwide, it appeared to the court that the abortion reform movement had significant public backing.[18]

In some ways, it did.

Roe v. Wade was the culmination of more than a decade of activism and political reform at the statewide level; more than 16 states had liberalized their abortion laws before *Roe*. However, what might have seemed like a long struggle for the abortion repeal activists who were working in the trenches didn't feel that way to many Americans. There continued to be a significant disconnect between the abortion activists and other Americans, many of whom were taken by surprise when *Roe* became the law of the land.[19]

The Pro-life Backlash

If abortion conversations opened during the '60s, they narrowed after the 1973 *Roe v. Wade* Supreme Court decision. A powerful opposition movement rose up practically overnight.[20] What no one could have predicted, according to Kristin Luker in her book *Abortion and the Politics of Motherhood*, was that "the *Roe* decision would mobilize a new and much stronger opposition to abortion reform."[21] Luker's work to chronicle the rise of the pro-life movement shows that *Roe* was a major wake-up call. One activist said the decision was "like a bolt out of the blue."[22] Luker wrote that for many pro-life people it seemed "the Court had suddenly and irrationally decided to undermine something basic in American life and they were shocked and horrified."[23] She noted, "Almost and without exception, [pro-life activists] reported that they became mobilized to the cause on the very day the [*Roe*] decision was handed down."[24]

Since *Roe*, thousands of laws and policies designed to restrict access to abortion have been presented to voters in local and statewide elections and introduced in state legislatures. The laws, despite significant pro-choice efforts to fight them, have been overwhelmingly successful, especially recently.

If abortion had been an open secret, a necessary evil, accepted yet not talked about before *Roe*, then the Supreme Court decision would have been seen as validating something that was already happening. Instead, there was a massive, concerted effort to "roll back the clock," as pro-choice activists would later call pro life activism.

While abortion is often considered a "women's issue," it must be understood that women were just as divided over abortion as anyone else. Both Judith Blake's look at public opinion polling in the 1960s and Kristin Luker's research on the pro-life movement in the 1980s revealed that many women opposed abortion. The pro-life activists who were politicized by *Roe* considered abortion the taking of a human life, and while they might accept that abortion was sometimes medically necessary, they also believed it was wrong. Most significantly, they believed that everyone shared this view. When *Roe* revealed that this wasn't the case, it came as a huge shock.

If *Roe* was the result of organizing and activism on behalf of women in need of safe, accessible abortions after decades of unspoken social acceptance, it was also an opportunity

for a long-overdue public conversation about how our society values the human fetus. But instead of open dialogue,
a brand-new cultural conflict emerged: the rights of the
woman were pitted against the rights of the fetus.

Frances Kissling, former president of Catholics for Choice
and the founder of the National Abortion Federation, discussed how this conflict became a fundamental challenge
for pro-choice activists in her 2004 groundbreaking article
"Is There Life After Roe?" Kissling asked, "Are we not capable of walking and chewing gum at the same time; of valuing life and respecting women's rights?"[25]

The shock and confusion in reaction to the Supreme
Court's apparent attack on pro-life values and traditions were
powerful and understandable. However, accounting for how
that outrage has been sustained with such dramatic impact
for so long requires more explanation. Luker pointed out
something unique about the commitment of pro-life activists: "The willingness of pro-life people to vote becomes
important. Because they are part of a very small proportion
of citizens who vote regularly, their opinions are weighted
more heavily than the opinions of nonvoters. And because
they also vote during primaries, where turnout is usually at
its lowest, their votes can often eliminate candidates who
do not have pro-life views."[26]

Bringing abortion issues directly to voters proved a winning cultural and political strategy for the pro-life movement in the decades after *Roe*. According to a Guttmacher
Institute report, more restrictions on abortion were passed
in two recent periods than in the previous decade com-
bined—from 189 restrictions between 2001 and 2010 to 205
abortion restrictions between 2011 and 2013.[27] The report

characterizes more and more states as "hostile" to abortion (up from 2 to 22 states in 13 years) and fewer and fewer states as "supportive" (down from 17 to 13).[28]

In 2013, 10 states enacted 16 measures to increase access to abortion. California enacted more liberal laws than any other state in 2013, with 4 laws. Compare that with the pro-life efforts the same year: 24 states enacted 52 measures to restrict access to abortion; Arkansas enacted the most restrictive legislation in 2013, with 8 laws. Oklahoma enacted 5 restrictive laws, and Missouri and North Dakota each enacted 4 restrictive ones.

According to the Guttmacher report, "States have constructed a lattice work of abortion law, codifying, regulating and limiting whether, when and under what circumstances a woman may obtain an abortion."[29] The laws cover issues such as the following:

- Who is legally allowed to perform an abortion (a licensed physician or nurse practitioner?)?

- At what stage of pregnancy can a person get an abortion?

- What type of government funds can be used to cover the cost of an abortion?

- What type of information are women required to receive prior to an abortion?

- What is the amount of time someone has to wait to get an abortion after she receives mandated information?

- What is the legal role of parents in the decision-making process of their minor children?

The opponents of many of these laws point out how the restrictions and mandated information were not created to assist women going through abortions but rather to create a series of legal, logistical, emotional, and geographical hindrances in obtaining an abortion. A significant amount of the information and counseling isn't scientifically or medically necessary, and at worst, it is factually inaccurate or grossly misleading. For example, some states are required to tell women that abortion can increase the risk of breast cancer, a myth that has been repeatedly disproved by the scientists who study cancer.[30]

Public policy and debate haven't been the only tactics of the pro-life movement to reduce abortions in the United States. Carole Joffe wrote about the devastating impact of violence against abortion providers in her book *Dispatches from the Abortion Wars: The Costs of Fanaticism to Doctors, Patients and the Rest of Us*. Since 1977, Joffe said, pro-life activists have committed "8 murders, 17 attempted murders, 41 bombings, 100 butyric acid attacks (butyric acid is a very foul-smelling agent), 175 arsons, and 656 alleged arson threats" against abortion providers.[31]

As a result of this onslaught of restrictions and the impact of antiabortion violence, the legal landscape of abortion access is different from county to county and state to state. As many pro-choice activists point out, abortion may be legal because of *Roe v. Wade*, but pro-life activists are doing their best to make it practically inaccessible.

Pro-choice Turn to the Right

In the 1980s, the political tide turned against the liberal social movements of the 1960s and '70s. It wasn't just the pro-life backlash to the *Roe* decision. The 1980s showed a growing trend toward more conservative social policies, especially when it came to crime.

For example, over a 30-year period, America's prison population grew from 300,000 to more than two million, making the United States the country with the highest incarceration rate in the world, "surpassing those in highly repressive regimes like Russia, China, and Iran."[32] Today, the United States imprisons more of its black population than South Africa did even at the height of apartheid. The racist outcomes of incarceration are a result of policies that were enacted in the '80s, many of which are attributed to President Reagan's War on Drugs, which implemented dramatic shifts in arrests and minimum sentencing guidelines for even nonviolent offenses, such as drug use and possession.

Pro-choice groups adapted to this increasingly conservative political climate.

Hoping to survive the times, the biggest, most well-known, and most influential pro-choice groups—such as NARAL and Planned Parenthood—found hope in aligning their missions with conservative ideas. They stopped talking about abortion and started talking about "choice," believing that a winnable strategy could be found in focusing on the private right to choose abortion rather than the feminist goal of increasing access to abortion services.

It started in 1986. In Arkansas, a state constitutional amendment was proposed to limit abortion funding, and it included a declaration of the rights of the unborn. The pro-choice coalition working in opposition to Amendment 65 didn't believe they had enough votes to win and were looking desperately for a way to make their message mainstream. In his book *Bearing Right: How Conservatives Won the Abortion War*, Slate journalist William Saletan recounted what happened next: Pro-choice leaders looked for ways to apply popular assumptions to abortion. Specifically, they sought to connect the right to an abortion with the fears and documented resistance of white southerners to any outside attempts "to confiscate their firearms or bus their kids to black schools."[33]

The pro-choice coalition won, narrowly. Amendment 65 was defeated. It was the first time a pro-choice political victory was due to alignment with a conservative political agenda.[34] Saletan pointed out that the decision created a "mutant version of abortion rights as a viable alternative to the feminist, egalitarian version originally envisioned by pro-choice activists."[35] Their southern strategy wasn't without opposition. NOW and the ACLU were critics of this approach, and many women leaders of color who were advocating for an increased government role in facilitating access and choice were understandably frustrated by the message. Despite criticism, the trend toward reframing abortion within a conservative antigovernment "keep your laws off my body" approach grew rapidly.[36]

The following year, NARAL abandoned its plans to address the abortion-access issues of poor women in order to take on a new political battle: defeating Reagan's Supreme Court nomination of Robert Bork. The political consultant behind the defeat of Amendment 65, Harrison Hickman, teamed up with NARAL President Kate Michelman for the all-hands-on-deck pro-choice campaign, creating a partnership that, according to Saletan, was the "most important turning point in the debate since *Roe*."[37] Given the power and influence of NARAL, the partnership between Hickman and Michelman solidified the pro-choice movement in a fundamentally conservative framework.

At that year's NARAL national conference, Michelman declared a "state of emergency" and addressed the "crisis" that Bork's nomination represented to women's rights and civil rights. Her original keynote was discarded, and she never said what she had originally planned to convey: "It is also our job to remember [each] woman. It's not really even an argument, but a collection of stories—stories of women who have faced the abortion choice thoughtfully, painfully, and morally."[38] Instead, she emphasized constitutional ideas about what the government could not do, ideas that came directly from Reaganism.

The pro-choice movement has never left the state of emergency that Michelman first declared in 1986. Each passing year has brought a new crisis and more reasons to abandon long-term proactive strategies in favor of short-term defensive tactics.

In 1988, in the final weeks before the presidential election won by George H. W. Bush, Michelman said in a speech how important it was to "listen to the women. . . . The voices of women are as varied as the reasons abortions are sought."[39]

The Voices of Women: Abortion, in Their Own Words—a NARAL book containing stories of women describing their illegal abortions—was part of the push for a massive march on Washington planned for a few months after Bush's election. But in the hours before the march, against staff objections, the "millions of voices" message was discarded in favor of an antigovernment message on privacy.

NARAL printed "Who Decides: You or Them?" on posters and buttons that were distributed to the thousands of grassroots activists who descended on DC to stand up for abortion rights. Today, this same message—"Who Decides?"—is the slogan for the conservative, antigovernment Tea Party organization called Citizens for Self-Governance.

Saletan summarized the impact of Michelman's decision to move the message away from women's voices and toward privacy: "Only years later would pro-choice advocates realize that rallying support for privacy had been the easy part. *Privacy* was a popular word because it was empty. It could be filled with whatever the speaker or the listener valued. The struggle between the conflicting values of speakers and listeners, between liberal and conservative understandings of privacy, was just beginning."[40]

As the pro-life movement steadily—and confidently—brought its issues directly to voters, shaping attitudes and public conversations, the pro-choice movement took a different tack, reacting defensively to resist pro-life influence and accepting a fundamentally conservative framework for its messages. In 1989, the same year as the pro-choice march by half a million supporters in Washington, DC, the Freedom of Choice Act (FOCA), which would codify *Roe* throughout the nation, was introduced in Congress. FOCA was reintroduced in 1993, 2004, and 2007, but it has never passed. The movement successfully worked for the passage of the 1994 Freedom of Access to Clinic Entrances Act, which protects abortion clinics from terrorist attacks such as arson and bombings.

Predominantly, though, pro-choice strategies have focused less on voters and public conversation and more on influencing powerful people and institutions. For example, much effort is put into supporting pro-choice candidates running for office or those being considered for appointment to important federal positions, such as on the Supreme Court or in the US Department of Health and Human Services. There has been significant effort exerted to sway federal agencies toward greater reproductive rights and access, such as seeking FDA approval for reproductive technologies like the "morning-after pill" (taken after sex to prevent pregnancy) and the "abortion pill" (called RU-486 in France before it was approved in the United States as mifepristone); but while these strategies can—and do—significantly increase access to services for women, they do not require a vote of Congress or the public.

Despite the real medical advances that such efforts represent, these conversations about abortion are happening in government arenas invisible and inaccessible to many Americans. Understanding the inner workings of government process has become a job for educated, connected professionals; and while citizens can participate in theory—by submitting written comments or advocating with their representatives, for example—the burden for participation falls on individuals who educate themselves and on the associations and nonprofits who attempt to organize

change. Today, many in the growing field of open government are working to fix this engagement problem by finding creative ways to bring issues directly to the public for
their input and participation.

Only in the last few years have pro-choice activists found
new footing with proactive strategies to increase support
for abortion and access to services. California bucked the
trend of increasing restrictions by passing a law in 2013 that
allows nurse practitioners, physician assistants, and certified midwives—a few select types of medical professionals other than doctors—to perform surgical abortions. This
bill is in stark contrast to what happened across the nation.
According to the Guttmacher Institute, in 2013 alone, 473
restrictions to abortion were introduced and 68 restrictions
were enacted.[41] California's AB 154 was the *only bill to successfully expand access to abortion*. The coalition that spon-
sored and supported the bill included a significant number
of small organizations that were community based and/or
led by women of color, and not a single one of the big medical elite professional groups like ACOG or the AMA that
had originally backed *Roe*.

The mainstream pro-choice strategies remain—as Judith
Blake originally suggested in the 1960s—in the hands of the
elite, not the grassroots, though the issues are often fought
on behalf of the most vulnerable. But the reductionist ten-
dencies of the pro-choice movement did create opportunities
for others to expand their organizing and advocacy efforts,
often to great success. For example, a small group of women
leaders of color started to organize under the banner of
"reproductive justice" during the conservative '80s. Instead

of being focused on the single issue of abortion, or *choice*, these leaders linked a wide variety of issues—from prisoner rights and social safety net concerns to the rights of women of color to bear children—together to create a broader movement able to collaborate naturally with other social-justice movements. Early efforts led by people such as Loretta Ross and her organization SisterSong Women of Color Reproductive Justice Collective helped set the stage for a wide-ranging and effective new national movement.

Today, a multiracial coalition of organizations around the country work together to promote their reproductive-justice agenda, which, defined by Forward Together, one of the leading organizations, is this: "The complete physical, mental, spiritual, political, economic, and social wellbeing of women and girls. Reproductive justice will be achieved when women and girls have the economic, social, and political power and resources to make healthy decisions about our bodies, sexuality, and reproduction for ourselves, our families, and our communities in all areas of our lives."[42]

This reproductive-justice approach to the politics of abortion has a winning record. In addition to their leadership on the passage of California's 2013 law to increase access to abortion services, campaigns led by women of color have defeated proposals in Colorado to declare a fetus a person with individual legal rights and one in Albuquerque, New Mexico, that sought to make late-term abortions illegal. Despite their successes, many of these winning organizations struggle to gain the financial support and public awareness that their mainstream pro-choice peers enjoy.

The Pro-life Movement Adapts, Too

The pro-choice movement wasn't the only one to initiate a
change in tactics in the 1980s. The pro-life movement also
felt pressure to reach out and influence the mushy middle in
abortion politics—the vast majority of Americans who have
layered, nuanced values and beliefs about abortion that fall
somewhere between the extremes of "abortion on demand"
and "abortion is a crime."

If the pro-choice movement sought to connect its political goals with conservative fears, then the pro-life movement
realized that it needed to find a way to connect its political
position with social concern for women's rights and health.
In the decade after *Roe*, the pro-life movement began to
claim that abortion harms women by causing them severe
emotional stress, going so far as to name a diagnosis, *postabortion syndrome*, which it likened to the trauma experienced by victims of war, terror, and abuse.

Six years after a family therapist named Vincent Rue testified before Congress in 1981 about this alleged emotional
disorder, President Reagan asked C. Everett Koop, his anti-
abortion surgeon general, to investigate the psychological
harm of abortion. Koop found no such evidence and refused
to issue a report. However, he was critical of this new pro-
life strategy and warned his pro-life allies, "As soon as you
contaminate the morality of your stand by getting worried
about the health effects of abortion on women, you have
weakened the whole thing."[43]

Despite this setback, the idea gained steam, supported
financially by the Catholic Church, which began to provide
counseling to women to help them deal with the "aftermath"

of abortion in the '80s.[44] In 1985, an antiabortion activist named David Reardon turned to social science as a way to prove the emotional damage of abortion. Surveying women who participated in a group called Women Exploited by Abortion, he "found high rates of nervous breakdowns, substance abuse and suicide attempts. He presented this as proof of a national link between abortion and these conditions."[45]

Since then, Reardon has written several books, conducted numerous studies—some of which have been published in respected peer-reviewed medical journals—and helped spur a movement of women who feel they were harmed by their abortions. Norma McCorvey, the woman pseudonymously called Jane Roe, has since expressed regret over her role in legalizing abortion and has become a pro-life activist. In 2003, she sought to overturn Roe; she helped submit hundreds of affidavits from women who had had abortions, expressing their pain, and requested that the court protect other women from such difficult experiences. The hope of this new woman-focused arm of the pro-life movement was "a future in which millions of women and men with experience of abortion would express outrage, demand reform and file lawsuits that would bankrupt abortion clinics."[46]

The American Psychological Association jumped into the fray and began a serious look at the scientific literature. A 1990 article in *Science* concluded that the evidence does not show that abortion poses a psychological hazard for most women.[47] Two years later, Nada Stotland, a psychiatrist who served as vice president of the American Psychiatric

Association, concurred in an article for the *Journal of the American Medical Association*: "There is no evidence of an abortion-trauma syndrome."[48]

Just because abortion alone doesn't cause a mental illness or disorder does not mean that a woman's experience of abortion isn't emotional and that she isn't in need of more support and understanding. The question of women's emotional experiences could have opened the door to a new public conversation, sparking investigation, research, and opportunities for women to speak openly toward the goal of better understanding the emotional health impacts of abortion, and what could be done personally, medically, and socially to promote better outcomes. However, a new fight prevented this opening. Instead of women's rights versus the rights of the fetus, now emotions were the new battleground. In this case, it was a war over science: good science (which was pro-choice) showed that women were fine, and bad science (which was pro-life) showed that they weren't.

It's not that the scientific arguments are irrelevant, it's just that with each new abortion issue, the same types of people—the lawyers, lobbyists, doctors, and scientists—continue to be the voices on the issue, establishing the parameters of the debate and neglecting opportunities for women and men to speak for themselves.

Several more literature reviews have been conducted since then, all coming to the same conclusion: the experience of abortion alone doesn't cause a mental disorder.[49]

However scientifically flawed the claim that women are psychologically harmed by abortions, the continuing insistence that it does so has had an immense social and political impact on public perceptions. Support groups of all shapes and sizes have sprung up around the country to provide a network of services. Thousands of affidavits by women describing emotional harm from an abortion have been filed in legal cases across the country, efforts organized by many of the postabortion groups. By 2000, hundreds, if not thousands, of postabortion service providers were in churches, retreat centers, and crisis pregnancy centers across the country.

Even if the science is dubious, the fact that women seek and attend these retreats after an abortion cannot and should not be ignored or discredited. Clearly, a need for support and connection exists, and women will go where it's offered.

Postabortion counseling existed on the pro-choice side too, but barely. Anne Baker, the former director of counseling at the Hope Clinic for Women in Illinois (no relation to me), wrote several pamphlets acknowledging emotions after abortion. She was often referred to as the "gold standard" for counseling in the field. A group of clinic owners and managers who met twice a year and referred to themselves as the "November Gang" were also known for the counseling they provided patients before and after abortion. Still, a dozen pro-choice practitioners were no match for the vast network of services provided by the pro-life organizations around the country. Additionally, the pro-choice movement was extremely uncomfortable with admitting any negative emotional repercussions after abortion and instead relied primarily on scientific conclusions that "most women feel relief."

In 2011, a study out of Denmark was published in the *New England Journal of Medicine* that showed yet again that there is no scientific evidence to prove abortion causes mental

illness. While all this science may reassure a woman consid-
ering abortion who is worried about waking up one day with
a life-threatening illness like bulimia, alcoholism, or obses-
sive compulsive disorder, it does nothing to prepare her for
any sort of emotional impact—personal, family, cultural, or
otherwise. The scientific findings are inadequate for understanding the scope and depth of a woman's experience.

Given the conflict over abortion, and each side's approach
to addressing women's emotions in particular, opening
conversations comes with significant political baggage.
Since Exhale's founding, I've heard many versions of these
comments:

- "Exhale shouldn't talk about 'after-abortion' or 'posta-bortion' support."

- "I'm worried that your language will be co-opted or used against abortion."

- "Aren't you just promoting the idea that abortion harms women?"

- "Doesn't offering women support imply that women need it?"

- "You make stigma worse when you talk about emotions, healing, and counseling."

Notice that not a single one of these questions or comments is concerned with what a woman who has had an
abortion might want or need after an abortion. The concerns
are always with the potential negative political implications
on one side or the other of the abortion debate. Rarely does
someone imagine a political upside!

Exhale doesn't make up the fact that thousands of Internet searches for "after-abortion" and "abortion emotions" are made each month. It's also true that more people call our talkine than we have the capacity to talk to. The increase in new postabortion services and the increasing demand for Exhale's services and expertise demonstrate a broad need.

What Exhale knows to be true is that women who have abortions are reaching out in a number of ways, searching for resources, support, connection, and inspiration. They are taking action to find it. It's critical that we understand and best meet the needs that exist. If a woman is searching online for information about "support after abortion," we want her to find helpful and healing information and resources she can use—not be told that she shouldn't need help or that seeking support has a political price tag more important than she is. Certainly, anyone is free to perceive her requests however they want—whether as a threat to their political position or as a symbol of the woman's weakness—but we simply don't.

As long as women have abortions, they are going to have feelings about it. Whether their feelings are complicated, ambiguous, or clear, having them is a natural, normal part of being human. When we take the time to listen, the strictly enforced black-and-white parameters of the abortion debate crumble away beneath the weight of our messy truths.

There is far too much gray area to permit dogmatic positions.

Chapter 3

Listen and Tell Stories

The abortion wars have eroded more than America's political climate. The conflict has had a direct impact on women who have abortions; on their families, friends, and communities; and on public perceptions about the decisions and behavior that surround an abortion.

The pro-life messages about women who have abortions have been mixed. According to Joffe in *Dispatches from the Abortion Wars*, "Women getting abortions were a prime focus of the movement's wrath, demonized as 'murderers,' 'sluts,' and interestingly, 'lesbians.'"[1] When it comes to the fanatics, she's right. But there is also a huge network of pro-life support centers around the country that offer counseling and the chance to talk with others dealing with abortion experiences. Pro-life advocates don't get women in the door by calling them sluts or lesbians; they do it by promising to listen and care. They pledge compassion.

From the outside, the tone and messages of the pro-choice movement sound radical and feminist, but their roots are fundamentally conservative. The messages aren't inviting, warm, or loving to women and their families who feel isolated or shamed after their abortions, or to those who want to open up publicly about theirs. The bumper sticker and T-shirt slogans that the public most identifies with the pro-choice side include:

"Keep your laws off my body."

"My body. My choice."

"Don't like abortion, don't have one."

 "U.S. out of my uterus!"

"Not Your Decision. Not Your Body."

"It's Personal."

While obviously targeted at their opposition, pro-choice messages make it clear that abortion is a subject that is off-limits for conversation. Lacking heart and empathy, infamous slogans like "Pro-choice NOT Pro-abortion" subtly indict women who make the choice, suggesting that to be pro-choice is to accept abortion as a necessary evil. There is no invitation to listen to a woman without judgment, no offer of comfort or concern for a woman's wellbeing, and no encouragement for her to talk openly about an experience.

For decades, the mainstream slogans have relayed the same message: keep away and keep out. They could just as easily be applied to the Second Amendment right to bear arms, stand-your-ground laws, or states' rights to prevent the federal government from integrating white southern schools with black students. The need to keep abortion choices private has pushed personal stories under the rug of secrecy.

Natalia Koss Vallejo, one of the first women in the country to share her first-person abortion story publicly on national TV, in a 2010 MTV special called *No Easy Decision*, noted in her talks around the nation as a member of Exhale's Sharing Our Stories Tour in 2013, "I wasn't raised in a pro-life household. I was never told that abortion was wrong." She wondered, "Why did I feel like I had to keep it a secret?"

Dr. Tracy Weitz, a well-respected social scientist and the founder of Advancing New Standards in Reproductive Health (ANSIRH), which works to ensure that reproductive health care and policy are grounded in evidence, wrote about her hesitancy in pulling back the curtain on the private nature of abortion in a 2010 blog post about Koss Vallejo's TV appearance. Weitz worried that public storytelling "runs a dangerous risk of welcoming the observer into the couple's abortion decision. . . . We need to be careful about setting up or encouraging storytelling that leads the general public to believe that they get to arbitrate women's reasons for choosing abortion. It is a legal option, not a popularity contest."[2]

Weitz's concerns represent the apprehensions of many pro-choice activists who worry about the political impact of what women say out loud about their own abortions.

No one makes perfect decisions, and no choice is without its consequences, so if the human right to legally choose abortion hinges on every woman's total competence and certainty beyond a shadow of a doubt, free of any personal or social costs, then surely the right to abortion will always be under threat. Objective certainty is an impossible standard to maintain.

Real abortion stories are often clumsy, inconsistent, and murky, if not sometimes tasteless and tacky. This messiness is why Judith Blake promoted an elitist solution to the problem of illegality in the 1960s and why political leaders like Kate Michelman have, since the 1980s, kept their focus on privacy and government intervention instead of women's voices.

The fear of making private issues public is nothing new for social activists, even so-called progressive ones, nor is it wrong for them to be afraid. The impact of new voices is unpredictable. More public storytelling—if done ethically, organically, and authentically—can further complicate the political terrain around abortion, not simplify it.

In 1969, Carol Hanish wrote the manifesto "The Personal Is Political" in response to the criticism that she and her peers received for participating in consciousness-raising women's liberation groups. For "trying to bring our so-called 'personal problems' into the public arena—especially 'all those body issues' like sex, appearance, and abortion"—Hanish and the other women were accused (mostly by men, but also women) of "navel-gazing" and of not being "political."[3]

Despite the attacks, the consciousness-raising groups helped Hanish to discover that "personal problems are political problems." She advocated, like so many social activists of her time, that people with shared experiences and similar structural challenges—whether as women, blacks, immigrant farmworkers, or any other marginalized group—should come together, share their stories, and decide how to move forward together. Through consciousness raising, she found out how different it was to work with other women than to work on behalf of some other downtrodden and oppressed groups as she had done in her past activism. She wrote, "I am getting a gut understanding of everything as opposed to the esoteric, intellectual understandings and *noblesse oblige* feelings I had in 'other people's' struggles." With consciousness raising, she built power through shared experiences.

Hanish also expressed curiosity, rather than judgment, about women whom she deemed "apolitical," recognizing that "we who work full-time in the movement tend to become very narrow. . . . I think 'apolitical' women are not in the movement for very good reasons, and as long as we say 'you have to think like us and live like us to join the charmed circle,' we will fail."[4] Four decades later, she reflected on her article in a follow-up piece published in 2006 to clarify that she had used the term "political" to describe changing the power structure in relationship and culture, not just the narrow field of electoral politics.

The personal is certainly political—it's just that in practice, these ideas seem to have gotten reversed. Instead of personal experience shaping the political landscape, now the political landscape defines how women should express their personal selves, raising the question, will women's self-expression about their abortions help or hurt the cause?

When it comes to stigmatized or hidden issues such as abortion, there are few personal stories available in the public domain, putting each one at risk for becoming the defining symbol. For the people who tell those stories, there is often a pressure to represent the group, whether they want that burden or not. While repeal activist Cisler wrote in 1970 that she wanted women who had abortions to be perceived by the public as "shapers of their own destinies," this was more wish than reality. Hanish wrote about how she experienced the social pressure to use her voice for the good of the whole group: "As a movement woman, I've been pressured to be strong, selfless, other-oriented, sacrificing, and in general pretty much in control of my own life. To admit to the problems in my life is to be deemed weak. So I want to be a strong woman, in movement terms, and not admit I have any real problems."[5]

The need for women, especially the feminist activists who were trying to break free of centuries of women's repression, to be perceived as "strong" has had a significant impact on the types of political organizing strategies that women feel they can choose. There are some notable examples of feminists who practiced nonviolence and advocated for peaceful solutions to social conflict, such as Alice Paul and Barbara Deming, but they are not as well known as the famous male leaders, such as Mahatma Gandhi, Dr. Martin Luther King Jr., and Nelson Mandela, who used the vulnerability of their social and political positions to elicit empathy from the rest of the world.

This approach—revealing vulnerability in public as a strategy to mobilize allies to action—is not as viable for feminists and pro-choice activists, who must disprove the notion that they are naturally fragile, delicate, and in need of protection in order to be heard effectively. In an ironic and tragic twist, the social construct of feminine vulnerability has been quite successfully exploited by pro-life activists to prove that women who have abortions are, in fact, fragile and in need of government protection.

It is not yet clear whether it's possible for women to show their vulnerability about abortion publicly in an attempt to break down stigma and stereotypes without eliciting chivalrous or gallant behavior that seeks to protect or free them from any consequences.

Vulnerable Advocacy

The Feminism and Nonviolence Study Group, formed in England during the 1980s, observed that "when women group together to work for peace and disarmament, we are often portrayed as expressing our true nature, since women are said to be 'guardians of life on earth.'"[6] The study group noted that it was a challenge to hold "on to the value of nurturing and de-escalating conflict without being seen as 'traditionally feminine.'"[7]

This group struggled with whether nonviolence was traditionally masculine or feminine, and they actually perceived male suffering—such as being beaten or imprisoned for direct action against injustice—in the service of nonviolence as a "form of machismo." As feminists and peace activists, they saw nonviolence through multiple lenses, and they articulated an important dilemma that still pervades our thinking about women trying to achieve social change today:

Often the values and practices of nonviolence overlap with what could be called "traditional female qualities," which isn't surprising since they are both outside the dominant culture. . . . The danger is that in confronting our conditioning, we will discard much that is actually positive, simply because society ascribes it to women. In this way, the methods and values of nonviolence, with its connotations of acquiescence and passivity, could be rejected, too, since in patriarchal terms, they do not seem to be steps towards our liberation.[8]

But, the study group concluded, "the understanding of nonviolence as activity rather than passivity does link with feminist efforts to encourage women to be more assertive."[9]

The question of how different types of political action are perceived by others—whether as feminine or masculine, passive or assertive—matters to any group that is trying to break through stigma, stereotypes, and oppression, and it's one where there remains significant inner-group conflict. Nonviolence, in particular, is especially susceptible to these dilemmas and misperceptions.

The 2013 passing of iconic South African leader Nelson Mandela resurfaced decades of controversy over the role and purpose of violence—and nonviolence—for the liberation of oppressed people around the world. While feminists in England perceived male nonviolent leaders as practicing machismo, Ta-Nehisi Coates implied in a piece in the *Atlantic* that the external pressures on Mandela to take a stand against violence were based in white leaders' desires to see him as submissive—i.e., passive and feminine.

Coates reminded readers: "For most of American history, very few of our institutions believed that black people were entitled to the rights of other Americans. Included in this is the right of self-defense. Nonviolence worked because it conceded that right in the pursuit of other rights. But one should never lose sight of the precise reasons why America preaches nonviolence to some people while urging other people to arms."[10] He went on to quote James Baldwin, a black writer and activist: "The real reason that nonviolence is considered to be a virtue in Negroes . . . is that white men do not want their lives, their self-image, or their property threatened."[11]

Violence and nonviolence, then, have both been employed for liberation; and while violence is more easily understood and accepted as natural, nonviolence is far more complicated, perceived as both macho and feminine, assertive and passive, and it's a practice that can subvert the dominant racist paradigm while also upholding it.

Can nonviolent actions—such as sharing vulnerable personal stories to shed light on hidden experiences—by women disrupt sexism without perpetuating it?

There is great anxiety and fear about how women will be perceived by the public once they tell the full, unvarnished truth about their abortions outside the fortress of one camp or the other. Women will undoubtedly be criticized and attacked—not just for their stories but also for how they decide to share them, with whom, and for what purpose: Are women acting too strong or not strong enough? Does a woman sound too fragile and girly or inappropriately confident and gutsy? Is she propagating sexism or challenging it?

Both pro-choice and pro-life activists regularly try to relieve women of the burden of their own experiences—whether they want to protect women from the pain of having an abortion or from the pain that can come with speaking about it. As one pro-choice activist explained, her anti-stigma work is motivated by her desire to free women from the burden of speaking about their own experiences.[12]

To control and shape public perception of abortion, some pro-choice activists believe that the pro-choice movement should tell stories "of women as heroes, where it is their ability to act that deserves respect."[13] Others want to present women as "happy and normal" and suggest that "pro-choice activists can own the positive, simple story, that abortion is part of women's lives."[14] Pro-life activists, on the other hand, hope that women will speak to the pain and emotional trauma of their experiences to create a groundswell of opposition to abortion. Either way, both sides perceive personal stories as an opportunity for women to represent their side in ways deemed useful for larger political purposes.

This approach is not unique to abortion or to other stigmatized issues and identities; and the professionalization of social change, with its focus on policy making and legal advocacy, has meant that simple stories are preferred over more complicated ones.

Civil rights advocates have distanced themselves from "the most stigmatized elements of the community," wrote Michelle Alexander in *The New Jim Crow*, her groundbreaking book about the mass incarceration of black men in America, because they have found that they are "most successful when they draw attention to certain types of black people . . . and tell certain stories about them."[15] Advocates prefer to defend black people who "defy racial stereotypes, and they have exercised considerable message discipline telling only those stories of racial injustice that will evoke sympathy among whites."[16]

Professional advocates working on behalf of blacks and women suppress complicated personal realities and experiences in the name of liberation and justice.

While their ultimate goals may be in opposition, pro-choice and pro-life activists are aligned in their strategic approach to storytelling, believing that if they can just get women to say the right things about their own abortions, if they can mold the women's stories according to pre-established ideas about the goodness or badness of abortion, then their side will win. Both strategies jeopardize the power of those who have had abortions to shape perceptions and social attitudes about their own personal experiences. There's another really big problem with this approach. In a popular TED talk, Nigerian author Chimamanda Ngozi Adichie spoke eloquently of what happens when an entire group is represented by a single story.

Simply, "It robs people of dignity."[17]

Nonjudgmental Listening

At the turn of the millennium, women who had abortions were caught in the middle: for emotional support, they could turn to the strings-attached programs of pro-life groups that were against abortion, or they could tough it out on their own.

The strangest part of all this was how much the culture had changed, becoming more emotionally aware than ever before. The '90s saw a revolution of all things related to personal empowerment and pop psychology. People grew up watching shows like Oprah, where they learned the value and role of emotions in their lives. Self-help books on emotional intelligence, or emotional IQ, hit the best-seller lists, and people strived to increase their self-awareness. Emotions weren't just the domain of women, or exclusive to psychotherapy sessions either. Whether you just watched the latest blockbuster or had your first day at a new job, everyone wanted to know: how did you *feel* about it?

By 2000, thousands of women were having abortions every day. Women having abortions could probably repeat every political slogan from both sides, but it was still rare for them to talk with one another about this common thing that had just happened in their lives. Even more rare was the presence of personal stories in the public domain. Society was more emotionally enlightened at the turn of the 21st century, but the abortion conflict was living in the past.

While new methods of self-awareness and self-expression spread like wildfire throughout the culture, abortion was still presented by advocates in predominantly black-and-white terms. In the rest of their lives, women were getting positive messages about the value of being able to identify, express, and cope with a range of emotions. Keeping things bottled up inside and toughing it out was becoming a less acceptable way to deal with life's challenges as more and more people learned the benefits of expressing their emotions in healthy ways.

My cofounders and I didn't want women who had abortions to suffer the impact of stigma alone while the rest of the culture got in touch with their emotions and built support networks for every kind of life situation imaginable. We believed that a safe, confidential outlet to express their intimate thoughts and feelings about their abortions would promote their health and emotional wellbeing.

On January 7, 2002, Exhale got its first call to our after-abortion talkline serving the San Francisco Bay Area. It came from a father, a man who had recently learned about his teenage daughter's abortion and didn't know what to say to her. He wanted help to find the right words.

Hearing from men isn't unusual for Exhale. Since the talkline opened, male volunteers have served as counselors, and every year, about 8 percent of our calls are from men. This means that we've talked to nearly 1,000 men. Often, a man will call to find out how to best support the woman in his life who had an abortion, whether it's his daughter, his sister, his friend, or his intimate partner. Sometimes he may want to talk about what he's going through, too. Whether his emotions are similar to or different from a woman's, a man will receive the same kind of nonjudgmental support and respect from our counselors as a woman who calls.

Since its opening, the postabortion talkline has grown from a Bay Area bilingual service to a national multilingual one. People often learn about our service directly from their abortion providers, who give out our brochures and information in their waiting rooms or after-care packages. Increasingly, people find out about the talkline on the Internet, especially the callers who had abortions decades ago. Calling Exhale may be the first time a person has told someone about that long-ago abortion.

Exhale's volunteer talkline counselors have answered more than 13,000 calls. Most calls come from women in their 20s (the age group that gets the most abortions) who have had an abortion within the last year. Approximately 15 percent of talkline callers are significant others, the mothers, friends, and sisters of a woman who has had an abortion; and about 5 percent of calls each year are conducted by a volunteer counselor in another language, usually Spanish.

Rarely are callers looking to talk about the political landscape of abortion, and the specifics of the abortion process—the clinic, its staff, etc.—aren't a major theme, either. They call to talk about their life, their hopes and fears for the future, and the emotions surrounding their abortion. Overwhelmingly, callers express feeling isolated and alone. Whether they express sadness or grief, or confidence and relief, they question whether they are in fact "normal." Given so much political banter and so little personal expression, it should come as no surprise that there is little information for women and men to use to compare their own experiences of abortion. It is this urge to compare experiences with those of others that helps people to feel less alone despite social stigma.

It should come as no surprise that intimate relationships are a major topic on the talkline. Some women find that abortion can bring them closer to their partner—for example, Stephanie, who had an abortion when she was 24. Now in her 30s with two kids, she said,

---

I feel like it was a totally bonding experience [with my partner]. I felt so much more connected with him after [the abortion]. Just watching how supportive he was. I never once felt like he wasn't right there with me and supportive, emotionally and physically. That was a huge thing for our relationship.

Other women are in an unhealthy relationship, and the abortion can serve as a wake-up call about the need for change, as in the case of Sara, who remembers,

---

I was in a relationship with someone who was mentally abusive, and I had segregated myself from my family and friends. I was ashamed of the person I was

. . . I'm in a great relationship now. . . . My friends and family are proud of what I've become and have told me time and time again that what is in the past stays in the past because my life is much more valuable now.

It isn't just couple-type relationships that abortion touches; it also tests relationships with our families, friends, and other loved ones.

A few years ago, a colleague reached out personally. Her teenage son had recently gotten his girlfriend pregnant, and she had an abortion. My colleague really, really wanted to talk about this with her friends. It was something she had gone through with her son and his girlfriend, something she had opinions and feelings about. She hadn't had the abortion herself, but she was a part of the story, and she had her own experience to share. We brainstormed ways in which she could meet her needs for sharing without violating her son's trust.

Brainstorming possibilities is one of the many things that counselors do on the talkline with callers. Counselors work with callers to come up with postabortion healing rituals, ways to get to sleep at night, information on how to stay healthy and active, possible conversations to have with loved ones, and ways to get additional support, and they address many more challenges. Often a talkline caller knows exactly what she needs, and the counselor's job is just to be there and listen as she tells someone what she's going through.

One call came from a woman who used the talkline as one of her many methods of self-care. She had just gotten home from her abortion, and she told the counselor that she had arranged for a friend to be with her at the clinic. That friend had left, and she was waiting for another to bring over dinner. The next morning, she planned to meditate and go to her yoga class, and then she was probably going to call Exhale back. The woman knew herself incredibly well. She knew what to do when she faced life challenges. She knew how to build a network of support around herself. She called the Exhale talkline to share her plans, using it as one more tool in her toolbox of social support.

Another caller, Julie, described what happened from her end:

I honestly thought about hanging up the phone. I didn't know what to expect, who I'd be talking to. But when the counselor picked up the line and introduced herself, I totally lost it. It was the weirdest feeling: this total stranger, just saying her name and asking for mine, all of a sudden made me feel like she cared. I mean, she did. She wouldn't be volunteering to answer phone calls if she didn't. I kind of expected there to be some script. Some nice things she was supposed to say to me. But it never felt like that. It just felt like she really cared. She didn't ask questions; she just let me talk. And in the end, she told me that she wished other women could have heard what I said because it was so inspiring. I thought: "Me? Inspiring?"

In 2013, *New York* magazine had a cover article featuring the abortion stories of 26 women, many with their pictures and their names. Three of the women featured were from Exhale—one was a board member and two were pro-voice fellows. Jozen Cummings, who had written his story as a man with an abortion experience a couple of years earlier on his blog, wrote a response for the *Root* and invited men to share their experiences. He wrote that every single abortion decision involves a man and advised that men can have empathy because they've been through these decisions, too. He said that he hoped "more guys are willing to step up and interject some personal experience in the politics."[18]

It isn't always easy for a man to be involved during an abortion process and give the support that he wants to give or the support that a woman may need from him. Rachel remembers what happened when she got to the abortion clinic:

When I got there, the receptionist had me pay and fill out paperwork. She told me a million things, and I sat down with my boyfriend. He went up and asked if he could come with me. Of course, they said no. Of course, I cried. The only thing that had kept my head up through all of it was the knowledge that the love of my life would support me even in that room. I was beyond devastated.

Journalist Liz Welch tackled the issue of couples in a January 2014 article for *Cosmopolitan*. Even though abortion can "test a relationship, cement it, or end it," as Welch found, one woman who works in an abortion clinic and who sees men in her waiting room every day noted, "These men care deeply about the women getting an abortion. It's crucial to include their experiences in the dialogue about the procedure."[19]

After our talkline launch, many from the pro-choice side said they assumed that the service was there for the very few, very rare people who felt badly after an abortion. Clinic staff members who let us know how much they valued our service told us that they were giving our information to any woman who was crying after her abortion, making the assumption that everyone else was "fine." From our perspective, we were actually less worried about the women who felt comfortable and safe enough to cry in the recovery room of an abortion clinic; we were more concerned about the woman putting on a steely demeanor to get through it, only to go home alone with no one to talk to and no idea that support like Exhale's talkline was available.

While some people thought that only women who were really upset—those they imagined were from religious or conservative backgrounds—would need to talk about their abortions, one woman, a prominent, outspoken Bay Area pro-choice activist, shattered that belief. She revealed to me one day that she had been so upset after her second abortion that she didn't think Exhale counselors could handle it, so she never called.

For some, Exhale's talkline was there only for the few people who were really upset, and for others, the talkline wasn't equipped to handle those who were distraught.

Not only was Exhale up against the challenges of the abortion conflict and stigma, but we were also fighting upstream against misperceptions about mental and emotional health. Those who supported abortion often assumed that the experience was no big deal, judging those seeking help as weak, brainwashed by religion, or victims of antiwoman messages. Those who disagreed with abortion often believed that it must be so horrible that everyone should receive mandated counseling. While the rest of our culture was expanding its definitions of emotional wellbeing, women having abortions were being pigeonholed and stereotyped for how they felt after having one. They were either too sad or not sad enough.

As people become more open with their own stories, often the same polarizing political dynamics get reinforced. For example, women have intensified their differences by choosing to build support networks limited to one side—and one particular set of feelings—or another. I'mNotSorry. net was established in 2003 in response to "regretful women wailing about how they felt so guilty" as an exclusive site for women to share "their positive experiences with abortion."[20] Silent No More Awareness was launched to "break the silence about negative consequences" as a private club for those who regret their abortions.[21] Instead of creating communities designed to foster curiosity and understanding across different emotional reactions, postabortion groups are often formed because women have felt that their unique experience and feelings are being marginalized.

Many are frustrated that the way they feel about their own abortion, or what they have heard others in their own social circles say about their abortions, is not the dominant, accepted perception of what abortion is really like for everyone. For example, when an anonymous woman shared about her abortion in Salon in 2010, she wrote:

I woke up feeling damaged, empty, scared, guilty and in pain. The terms "pro-choice" and "pro-life" were emanating from the TV screen. They sounded reductive, glaringly inadequate. The word "abortion," fraught with shame and accusation, was being bandied about for pieces of political theater. The words "baby killer" were omnipresent, too. Although I didn't feel like a baby killer, like I'd killed my baby, I did feel partially dead.[22]

Another woman, Serai1 (a username), who also had had an abortion, responded in the comments:

Are we ever—and I mean EVER—going to see an article written by a woman for whom abortion was NOT "the hardest decision of my life"? Because I can assure you, there are thousands of women for whom this is not a hard decision, not at all. I was one of them. . . . In fact, in all my life, I've never known any woman who had an abortion who wrung her hands or agonized about it. They all considered their options and decided for abortion in a calm, reasonable manner.[23]

Angie Jackson live-tweeted her abortion in 2010, which made her one of the first to use social media to break through the privacy barrier and bring her unvarnished experience to the world.[24] Nelle-Yecats, a woman who has had an abortion, couldn't support Jackson. Commenting on a *Huffington Post* article about Angie, she wrote:

I cannot agree w/Angie & her sharing on-line w/the world about her decision to abort. I do not talk about my abortion & miscarriages much to anyone. It is painful. I carry it all close to my soul.[25]

Acknowledging how stigma and conflict conspire to separate women from each other, @abortioneers tweeted that it "can be hard to hear someone describe an experience you think of as 'yours' in a not-yours way." She continued, "After so long thinking yours was the ONLY story (or only one available), finding others and their stories is both a blessing and a challenge!"[26]

In the stigmatized climate around abortion, some women have spent decades feeling judged for their experiences. The lack of openness and public conversation has created a gaping need for many to hear others speak thoughts, feelings, and experiences that are similar to the ones they've held in their own hearts. Often, there is a corresponding need to see others who look like them, too, women who are from similar backgrounds, ethnicities, faith, families, and communities. Some experts who work in the field of stigma and storytelling believe that every individual listener in an audience needs a story that matches theirs in order to feel connected. Rather than narrowing down the abortion experience into one or two simple stories that everyone is supposed to relate to, what's needed is a huge range of different stories that reflect the diversity of women and their experiences.

In addition to more stories, we need more listeners. Pro-voice helps people take a stand to listen across their differences, to be empathetic instead of judgmental.

The Worst Thing About America

Journalist Hanna Rosin claimed in her book *The End of Men: And the Rise of Women* that in the last 30 years, economic changes have disproportionately benefitted American women, given that the service and information economies reward more "female" traits, concluding: "The post-industrial economy is indifferent to brawn." Rosin was harshly criticized, called both a "radical feminist" and "an antifeminist" for her ideas. "I am neither of those things," Rosin responded, "but my findings do herald both straightforward progress for women on some fronts and tremendous headaches on others."[27]

Jennifer Homans's review of Rosin's book in the *New York Times* illustrates the modern political dilemma of what happens when gray areas are exposed publicly: "This kind of argument seems carelessly apolitical, especially at a moment when we are faced with public officials actively working to undermine access to birth control, abortion, equal pay for equal work."[28] Rosin wasn't political enough. However, more dogmatic politics aren't always what's most useful for social change.

Erick Erickson, a conservative commentator and founder of the blog RedState, wrote in the political aftermath of the killing of Trayvon Martin, a black teenager in Florida, by

George Zimmerman while walking home from the store one night, that the "worst thing about America is the politicization of everything." He demanded to know "why the hell must I pick a side in the George Zimmerman trial? A 17-year old boy is dead and a man who may or may not be guilty of murder is on trial. . . . Why am I forced, as a conservative, to cheer for the guy who took his life?"[29] Erickson expressed frustration about how "I can't live my life constantly fixated on the political outrage of the day. . . . Truth is, there is more to life than politics."[30]

It isn't just conservatives decrying the problem of too much outrage and not enough humanity. Feminist and social-justice activists too are realizing that it's time for something else. After the *Nation* published its 2014 cover story titled "Feminism's Toxic Twitter Wars," showing how prominent feminists had been attacking each other online, two prominent leaders—Brittney Cooper and Samhita Mukhopadhyay, both featured in the article—wrote on Twitter about the need to "humanize and be compassionate." On the blog *Orchestrated Pulse*, RobtheIdealist said, "The aimless outrage has many social justice circles spinning their wheels and going nowhere."[31] Even Cecile Richards, president of Planned Parenthood, advocates for talking personally to get "these conversations out of the political realm and into people's real lives."[32]

Everywhere one looks, the problem of increasing political polarization is being pointed out as one of the major issues facing America today. Adam Liptak wrote in a 2014 *New York Times* op-ed that "for the first time, the Supreme Court is closely divided along party lines . . . [and] the perception that partisan politics has infected the court's work may do lasting damage to its prestige and authority and to American's faith in the rule of law."[33] Princeton University professor Christy Wampole, also in the *New York Times*, suggested ways to help people deal with it all, including "disregard" to avoid the psychological pitfalls of constant distress brought on by outrage politics. She advised, "Accrue your energies for better things."[34] CNN contributor Sally Kohn suggested a practice of "emotional correctness" in her 2013 TED Talk, noting, "You can't get anyone to agree with you if you don't listen to them first."[35] Even philanthropy is getting involved: the William and Flora Hewlett Foundation announced a new initiative in 2014 to focus on "alleviating polarization . . . a precondition for successfully addressing the other problems that bedevil us."[36]

There is growing discontent with the polarization of American politics. At the same time, efforts deemed not "political enough" are quickly targeted and attacked by those who care about equality and social justice.

Sheryl Sandberg, the Facebook COO who authored a 2013 book of advice for ambitious women titled *Lean In: Women, Work, and the Will to Lead*, received harsh criticism from activists working on feminist workplace issues. Anna Holmes, founder of *Jezebel*, called the reactions a "pile-on." "Critics," Holmes lamented in a *New Yorker* article, "seemed to come to their conclusions not as journalists but as activists."[37] Sandberg wasn't judged just for her arguments and advice but also on whether her life experience and personal story made her credible in the fight to improve the lives of working mothers.

Sandberg's book came on the heels of Anne-Marie Slaughter's treatise in the *Atlantic* titled "Why Women Still Can't

Have It All."[38] A former Princeton University professor and U.S. State Department director, Slaughter focused on the need to change complicated structural and policy issues, a position that seemed antithetical to Sandberg's advice on the ways that women could navigate and transform such obstacles through their own leadership, but together they offered the most expansive vision for change in decades.

When the media quickly pitted Slaughter and Sandberg against each other—the woman who finally admits she can't have it all against the one who says women must keep trying—they adhered uniformly to the underlying, ongoing story of what happens when women tell the truth about their own unique lives in the public sphere: they are judged primarily by the perceived value that their experiences and unique voice can bring to broader political goals.

Slaughter opened her article with a story about how she was finding it difficult to be away from her son and family while her career grew. She mentioned to a colleague that she wanted to write about this challenge in an op-ed but was told this wasn't a good idea. "You can't write that," her colleague said. "You, of all people." Slaughter knew that "what she meant was that such a statement, coming from a high-profile career woman—a role model—would be a terrible signal to younger generations of women." There could be unpredictable, perhaps uncomfortable, political consequences of telling her truth. Her colleague was right. Slaughter's article sparked a tremendous amount of controversy.

In this, Slaughter and Sandberg had a lot in common. In both instances, although for different reasons, the political implications of each woman speaking honestly about her own experiences as a professional working mother—in their case, superrich or just plain upper class—and the lessons she drew from them were too risky. Both were advised, privately and publicly, by other women that they should not bring their views to the public sphere. If the viewpoints of those with extraordinary privilege and economic means are too unsettling for public conversation, then imagine how unwelcome the opinions of women with far fewer advantages are.

And yet, despite the risks they knew were ahead of them, they did it anyway. Both Slaughter and Sandberg spoke publicly of their regrets and hard lessons learned, and by doing so they revealed their own unique vulnerabilities. They tried to communicate the true-life dilemmas of professional working mothers as they saw them, and they succeeded in complicating—and by that I mean furthering—the conversation over women and work with new realities, stories, ideas, facts, and concerns. Both opened up nuances and challenges never imagined when Betty Friedan published *The Feminine Mystique* in 1963, decades before Slaughter had the opportunity to rise to power in the US State Department and decades before Facebook, let alone the Internet, was around for Sandberg to run. The world had indeed changed, and the impact, leadership, and experiences of working mothers had changed it.

There should be no doubt that working mothers will change the world yet again.

Sandberg and Slaughter didn't shy away from the media storm or go hide under a rock once the controversy hit. Neither was perceived as a fragile flower, and they didn't warrant any government protection. Both came off as incredibly strong . . . and incredibly *ambitious* about their desire to make real, measureable social change. Maybe it was their obvious, forthright ambition that was their real political problem, given that ambitious women "often pay a social penalty," according to Sandberg's *Lean In*. Undoubtedly, each has become more resilient as a result of her time in the spotlight.

Resilience is also possible for women who have had abortions, whether it's their ability to get through them or their need to speak openly about them despite attacks from a judgmental culture. Women aren't so fragile that they can't be trusted to make the decision to begin with, nor do they need to be protected from the vulnerability that comes with sharing their personal stories publicly.

No one knows more about building personal resilience than Hillary Clinton, who in a speech to New York University students in February 2014 advised that they develop a thick skin. But even more important than plain old resilience, she said, women need to be true to themselves in public life, "without it making you less authentic or undermining your confidence, and that is not an easy task."[39]

Women need to be true to their authentic selves when they tell their own stories publicly despite the reality of increasing political polarization. Pro-voice makes it possible to build the resilience needed to influence public conversations with their voices.

Ethical Storytelling

Monica first came to Exhale as a caller to our talkline. Later, she became a volunteer and then a part-time staff person. When she responded with interest to the e-mail I had forwarded to our volunteers from a documentary filmmaker looking for women to tell their abortion stories on film, I was surprised. Monica was known for being quite shy. Still, she was committed to helping other women not feel so alone, so she was willing to step outside her comfort zone. I gave her information about the project and wished her luck.

A few months later, her story was turned into a three-part web video series. Monica's was one of many stories to put a human face on the political issues at stake in the 2008 presidential election. Watching the first two videos online, I was blown away. Monica looked so peaceful and self-assured, and her words were her own. I could see her in the video. But the third video concluded with her saying, "In the end, I felt relief." I knew a lot about Monica and I had heard a lot of her story, but those weren't words I'd ever heard her say before. When I asked her about it, she said she had felt pushed and prodded into saying certain things, and the nuances and complexity of her story—showcased in the first two videos—got boiled down into the most basic of pro-choice talking points.

As part of her own self-care, Monica never watched any of the videos. It was enough for her that she'd done them. Her decision was all well and good until one day when she was on YouTube, and her own video popped up on the screen. She saw all the mean, horrible things that had been said about her in the comments, and she was devastated. She called Exhale immediately and asked for the video to be taken down. We got her in touch with the producers, and they took it down right away.

I was horrified. Though the film wasn't our project, I felt that Exhale had let Monica down in some way. What, if anything, should we have done differently? What was our responsibility in this situation? What was hers? What about the producers and the filmmaker, and what about YouTube? One woman's decision to share her personal story in a pubic manner so that she could help break down the isolation felt by other women after an abortion had turned into something much more complex.

Needing to find answers to this dilemma was what launched Exhale headfirst into storytelling. We saw the writing on the wall. Women who had had abortions—our callers and our community—were going to be asked more and more to share their stories for a whole range of purposes. We needed to explore what impact the explosion of digital media and social networks would have on women sharing their stories. Most important, what would be the impact of storytelling on their emotional wellbeing and their ability to find support?

We weren't the only ones thinking about storytelling. It was taking off. It was a storypalooza. A storyfest. Everyone and her brother was talking about stories, yet at first glance, most of what we saw in the progressive, nonprofit sphere was about how to package personal stories for fundraising and persuasion purposes. The term *narrative* was used interchangeably with other communications strategies such as *framing* and *messaging*. There appeared to be little comprehension of the impact of stigma on storytelling, nor any mention about what was so necessary for storytelling to work: listening.

Those who were most concerned about the problem of abortion stigma seemed the least informed about how it operated, often confusing normal, natural human emotion with the negative impact of stigma. For example, some pro-choice activists implied that if a woman felt sad after her abortion, her sadness and grief *must* be the result of stigma, or antiabortion, antiwomen messages, instead of the actual experience of abortion itself. In this particular worldview, no "negative" feeling would be consistent with abortion, and in a stigma-free world, women would experience only "positive" feelings like relief or gratitude after their abortions. Many espoused the belief that if more women just "came out" about their abortions, then stigma would go away, along with any difficult feelings. Abortion would be about as emotional as getting a mole removed.

In contrast, the pro-life side believed that *only* negative emotions were consistent with abortion because it was always the wrong, sinful choice. In their worldview, any positive emotions a woman expressed were deemed the result of her emotional denial and, often, her rejection of God's forgiveness, which many believe is the only way to healing and wellbeing after an abortion.

Exhale does not share either perspective. First, we believe women when they express their feelings after an abortion, whatever they may be. Each woman is the expert in her own life, and we can validate her emotions without judging the rightness or wrongness of her personal reaction. Additionally, we understand stigma to be the barrier that prevents a woman from freely expressing herself, whatever her feelings may be, and prevents her from connecting with other women who have experienced the same thing. The truth is, to be "stigma free" is not to be free of emotion but rather to feel confident in one's ability to express and cope with a full range of natural emotions. And, while seeking forgiveness from God can bring peace to some women who have abortions—a process that should also be respected without judgment—it is certainly not the only way to wellbeing.

Melissa Harris-Perry (formerly Harris-Lacewell) spoke persuasively in a 2009 speech before Planned Parenthood San Diego about shame, saying that the answer to shame is not to push people to come out and that instead the goal should be to soothe.[40] She said that it's easy to further shame those who choose to keep their experiences secret.

The narratives of stigmatized groups are easily judged and dismissed as irrelevant. "When members of lower status groups tell stories," wrote Francesca Polletta in *It Was Like a Fever: Storytelling in Protest and Politics*, "they are more likely to be tagged [negatively]." Polletta suggested that, for example, if a person of color shares her story, the "reasonableness, generalizability, and political seriousness" of her story may be questioned,[41] whereas if a white person shares one, it is more likely that hers will be taken seriously.[42]

We wondered what this bias meant for women who had had abortions and who came from all backgrounds, races, and ethnicities. Could Exhale further stigmatize women who, for any reason, didn't want to come out about their abortions? We had already witnessed how some stories and feelings expressed by women after abortion were not taken seriously, even by their own advocates. And there was real danger in "coming out." Exhale's volunteers heard from hundreds of women on our talkline about the negative impact of sharing their abortion experiences with friends or family—from being harassed in the workplace to being cut off by loved ones, practically excommunicated.

Ethically, Exhale could not suggest that women take risks we knew to be potentially dangerous, nor could we serve as their protector, shielding them from harm. Instead of trying to fix this dilemma, we chose to explore the gray areas of storytelling. We sought to find out what motivated women to share their stories, what they needed to feel heard when they did, and how to promote their wellbeing when they took big risks.

The dilemma was an opportunity to engage with our community and discover new insights together. We initiated a series of pilot projects, with women as our partners, to find the opportunities in the challenges of storytelling. As we invited women to participate, we were upfront about the issues we had identified and made sure they were coming in with eyes wide open. They signed on because they saw the challenge, too, and they wanted to be a part of figuring it out. As collaborators, we could explore the possibilities together.

Over the course of a few years, Exhale experimented with a wide variety of storytelling projects, achieving varying degrees of "success." All were successful in that we learned something new as a result of our efforts, but not all of them were endeavors worth a long-term investment of our resources. Our experiments and lessons learned included these:

> *Monica's story with the documentary filmmaker.* It wasn't enough for Exhale just to connect women with people who wanted to broadcast their abortion stories. Women needed to be empowered to have a say in how their stories would be used and needed to be supported when their stories elicited backlash.
>
> *Digital stories.* Given Monica's experience, we sought a method for women to tell their own stories, in their own words, rather than rely on someone else's

interpretation. In partnership with the Silence Speaks program of the Center for Digital Storytelling, five women each made their own three-minute video about their abortions through an intensive multiday workshop. One major lesson learned here was that as willing as the women were to have their stories spread far and wide, they didn't want the stories uploaded on the Internet. We learned that there is a distinction between being public and being "super-public"—i.e., shareable on the Internet.

Exhale Online Community. Run by Exhale for three years, this private online community was made available to talkline callers who wanted to talk with others who had had abortions. Potential members were screened by talkline counselors, referred, and given a private access code. While we were concerned that the high level of security might be a barrier to participation, we found that it provided a significant sense of safety. Members shared openly with the community about their incredibly private stories, knowing that they were protected from the public at large.

Distributing stories. Exhale presented the digital stories in events around the country and began sharing abortion stories on our website and through social media. Immediately, it was obvious that live audiences responded quite differently to the stories depending on whether the storyteller was present—more open and welcoming to the message if the woman was there, more judgmental if she wasn't. They began to judge the craft and artistry of how the story was told, rather than engage with the story itself. The same was true online. We saw that the ways that people interpreted stories were often very different from the ways that the story-teller had intended them. If a woman was trying to articulate the gray areas of her experience, people online were quick to find their own moral to her story, often labeling her. For example, one woman's story of over-coming adversity, which felt empowering to the story-teller, was often perceived as sad, leading the audience to pity the woman and her journey, not respect her.

Storytelling is much trickier than just getting more women to do it, and its impact on audiences is complicated. Because stories are so personal and emotional, people have gotten savvy about the intentions of someone who tells her story. "We are wary of listening to stories that we think are being told to manipulate our emotions or push us to believe a certain way," says Polletta.[43]

For example, Mira Ptacin wrote about her abortion in "Un-bearing," a poignant article for *Guernica*. Her readers, captivated by the power of her emotions, found themselves feeling emotional, too, and were either inspired or angry about where those feelings took them. "Thank you for such a heart wrenching illustration of why women must have the right to choose," wrote one reader in response. But another commented, "It is sad to see a woman who is obviously a gifted writer use her talents to evoke emotions that would excuse taking the life of another innocent human being."[44]

After reading Ptacin's emotional story, people either embraced or rejected it, based on their beliefs about her reasons for telling it. "On the other hand," says Polletta, "ambivalent stories, stories with no clear moral agenda, invite the listener to imagine themselves in the story. True engagement happens when the listener can see multiple outcomes for a story and is able to come to their own conclusions."[45]

When a woman shares her abortion story, a listener needs to be able to place herself in the woman's shoes and be given the freedom to consider how she might deal with the same situation. It's possible that given the same set of circumstances, the listener would go in a completely different direction. She could see other options, other paths not taken, and she might experience different pressures or emotions. It is this imagining of oneself in the situation that forms the real connection between the storyteller and the listener, not that the listener agrees with the storyteller's decisions or conclusions.

The mistake that feminists have made about bringing stories into the public sphere, said UC Berkeley law professor Kathryn Abrams, is to assume that "simple, linear narratives in which the moral is unequivocal and the experiences depicted are easily generalizable are the most effective in gaining recognition for needs that are currently ignored."[46] For example, when an advocate shares a simple story of the obstacles a woman has undertaken to get an abortion, it is clear to the audience that the advocate is trying to demonstrate why such legal restrictions are bad. Audiences often resist being led in a particular direction, sometimes because they have other beliefs, but often simply because they don't want to be dictated to or emotionally manipulated. Instead, stories that demonstrate a woman's ambivalence and that are specific and particular to her, and no one else, may be better at engaging an audience.

"Good stories," says Poletta, "are not necessarily simple ones, with unambiguous moral punch lines. Rather, narrative's power stems from its complexity, indeed, its ambiguity."[47] The benefit of narrative, especially for communicating across difference or conflict, is that stories can open imagination and move people out of their stuck positions. The more ambiguous a story, the more likely that people from a range of viewpoints will be able to imagine themselves in the story's context.

There is a difference between stories designed to open conversations and those designed to close them, according to Sam Gregory, the program director for the international human rights organization WITNESS. Sharing an ambiguous story welcomes people into conversation, into relationship, into engagement with you. Sharing a story with a clear-cut direction and moral outcome, on the other hand, closes a conversation.[48]

Polletta outlined a few key strategies for utilizing ambiguous stories for cultural change:

- *Use words that have multiple meanings to forge coalitions across difference.* For example, there can be many interpretations for how to "support women after abortion," whereas phrases like "defending a woman's choice" or "helping women recover from abortion's aftermath" signal a fixed political perspective. "Black lives matter," the phrase created to raise awareness about the extrajudicial killings of black people, is a perfect example of a unifying statement.

- *Play with the point of view of the storyteller so that her intentions are muddled.* For example, when students participated in lunch-counter sit-ins during nonviolent organizing in the South, they often talked about their actions as "spontaneous" when they were anything but. It was more effective for them to describe their emotion leading them to action rather than their careful strategic planning. Telling their story this way could inspire others to let their emotion move them to action.

- *Combine words, ideas, and emotions that don't usually go together.* When domestic-violence survivors talk about feeling destroyed by their abusers yet still being in love with them, readers must try to understand what's happening at a deeper level. The listener is forced to think beyond her own experiences. For example, "I think I would hate someone who hurt me. How could I still love him?"

Listening and storytelling are empathetic practices. Yet their purpose is not solely to generate empathy for oneself or one's stigmatized group. Instead, listening and storytelling are most effective when the stigmatized group utilizes these strategies to invite conversation and engagement—including from those who oppose or oppress them. When women who have abortions and other marginalized groups use these strategies, they shift from being victims of stigma to being proactive shapers of their own culture.

Finding Kindred Spirits

We got lost driving in the dark on our way to the large new Episcopal church on a hill in Austin, Texas. The fellows, we Exhale staff members, and the three-person documentary film crew following the fellows on the 2013 Sharing Our Stories Tour all found our way to a back room that was often used to distribute food to local needy families. Turns out there were more of us than there were participants. It was the smallest event of the tour. There were just three people in the audience.

It may also have been one of the most inspiring. It was organized by an older pastor named Linda (not her real name), who was just months away from her dream of being ordained. She had persuaded two of her friends to attend. It was held at a beautiful new church miles away from Linda's own because she feared repercussions for hosting the event. Since the Episcopal Church elected its first openly gay bishop in 2004, it has been deeply divided. Many congregations left the fold and formed a separate association to distance themselves from what they saw as the problem of growing gay acceptance. For over a decade, the internal conflict among Episcopalians has incited animosity and distrust and fractured many longtime relationships. Linda's tiny conservative rural church in the heart of Texas continues to be deeply divided.

Despite her fears about what could happen to her ordination and her relationship with her congregation, Linda knew that abortions took place in her community. And the question for her wasn't whether or not it was wrong, but whether or not it could be talked about. "There are a lot of secrets" that happen at church, one of Linda's friends observed. The three women who attended the pro-voice event came because they didn't want the women who were a part of their church community to feel as if they had to keep their abortions hidden. They wanted the women to feel supported, accepted, and loved.

These three women had had enough of secrets and conflict. "I have beloved community on both sides," Linda said. "I want us to be able to talk about our differences."

The conversation lasted hours, going far over the time scheduled. Secrets and inspiration were shared. It was clear that despite how different we looked on the outside, we had a lot in common. Linda and Exhale were engaged in the same kind of work, in our own ways. We were both seeking to stay in relationships with our friends on both sides of hostile divides while taking big risks to find common ground. We were kindred spirits.

Sometimes that's all that's needed—to know you're not alone, that others share the same desires and the same commitment to do what others think is impossible. Just as women who have had abortions can find solace in connecting with other women to share stories, we found comfort as pro-voice advocates in knowing that there were others who believed in transforming conflict into peace. We swapped our pro-voice stories.

In the end, Linda invited us to hold hands, and she prayed for us all.

We have to look for stories and people, like Linda, in the hidden places. We can't just expect them to find us. This is why seeking out the gray areas is important. They open the door for conversations that you didn't even know you needed, insights that didn't exist until you took the risk to find them. Sharing ambiguous stories creates the possibility for a room full of strangers with different values and beliefs about abortion—or a room with a few unlikely allies—to come together and feel connected. In a nation where it's often assumed that the conflict over abortion is here to stay, the idea that peace is possible is radical.

Over a decade ago, the feelings that follow an abortion were either politicized or ignored. While the tendency to label postabortion feelings and support services as either helping or hurting the cause of abortion rights is still strong, it's no longer the only response. New services, training, and public messages from both the pro-life and pro-choice sides have developed to address the broad spectrum of emotions and the different ways that women can find support.

We have yet to see if those with similar goals, who find themselves on different sides of the political aisle, will make the leap to change the culture together.

Sticky challenges like these are better addressed when communities and organizations collaborate in the process of discovery. Listening and storytelling, when done to open conversations rather than close them, help move people away from their fixed positions. When people are encouraged to come to their own conclusions, they are more willing to engage in conversations that can lead to agreement among differences. Regardless of the outcome, the process—of listening and storytelling—is fundamentally different from the warlike political battles that have dominated the abortion conflict, leaving room for people to be respected and respectful.

Trusting strangers to find their own moral within your personal story is hard to do. Openness and ambiguity can feel like an invitation to be hurt and disrespected. It might even seem like a sacrifice, or a position of weakness, to withhold your own opinion in the service of inviting another's engagement. Yet it is precisely this vulnerability that is so powerful for generating more love and compassion.

Chapter 4

Embrace Gray Areas

The abortion conflict causes separation that damages human dignity, placing women having abortions in the cross-hairs of enemy thinking. But this conflict isn't the first in human history. There is a lot to be learned from past and current endeavors to inspire people to create connections and rise above hostility.

Hope is everywhere. By all accounts, humans have overcome some of their most divisive behaviors, improving the quality of life for most people around the world. In nearly every metric available to assess violence, economic indicators, and gender roles, studies show that we are living in a fundamentally better and more equal time in history.

Steve Pinker, a professor of psychology at Harvard University, is one of many prestigious authors who have studied this trend. In his 2011 book *The Better Angels of Our Nature: Why Violence Has Declined*, Pinker concluded, "Believe it or not—and I know that most people do not—violence has declined over long stretches of time, and today we may be living in the most peaceable era in our species' existence." Pinker made the case that our brains have been shaped by evolution, predisposing us to violence (our inner demons) but also to peace and cooperation (the better angels of our natures). One reason Pinker gave for why violence has decreased is the process of feminization and the increase in women's rights.[1]

America, too, has improved itself many times over its history.

The historian Gordon Wood has written about how America transformed itself from a colony of the British monarchy into an independent democracy. "The problems of American politics were social," he explained in *The Radicalism of the American Revolution*, arguing, "All social changes have been social and cultural."[2] The American revolutionaries transformed the "relationships that bound people to each other," a change that was as "radical and revolutionary as any in history."[3] The change wasn't sudden. "Republicanism did not replace monarchy all at once. It ate away at it, corroded it, slowly, gradually, steadily."[4] But once started, the "idea of equality could not be stopped. It tore through American society and culture with awesome power."[5]

America was created out of this powerful social movement, led by revolutionaries who advocated "self-love as necessary to the support and happiness of the world,"[6] who extended charity to "our enemies as well as our friends,"[7] who believed that "one's humanity was measured by one's ability to relate to strangers, to enter into the hearts of even those who were different."[8]

It wasn't the only time these ideas shaped the direction of our nation.

The civil rights movement also pushed for a social change in relationships, calling on Americans to be the best versions of themselves in order to step into a higher plane of humanity. Civil rights activists who believed in the power of nonviolence went far beyond a basic rejection of inequality. They had the audacious belief that they—the powerless, the oppressed, and the poor—could lead their communities *and* their oppressors toward a shared vision of equality and justice. They accepted leadership responsibility for shaping the future of the country despite their lower social positions.

Nonviolence, according to the Pulitzer Prize–winning historian Taylor Branch, is the "orphan of democratic ideas."[9] Even during the heyday of the civil rights movement, the practice of nonviolence was not easy, and it was always controversial. Yet, Branch wrote in *At Canaan's Edge: America in the King Years, 1965–68*, "the nonviolent civil rights movement lifted the patriotic spirit of the United States toward our defining national purpose."[10]

It was a tough sell. The bitterness and pain of Jim Crow and the incredible obstacles led many to abandon nonviolent ideas and seek resolution by other means, but Dr. Martin Luther King Jr. held firm. He encouraged his followers to "not lose faith in our white brothers."[11] The commitment to hold compassion for enemies remains unusual in American culture, but it is not without precedent. The people who choose forgiveness over revenge open minds and raise expectations for how to deal with pain, violence, and anger in creative ways that can affirm and sustain dignity.

Sujatha Baliga told the *New York Times Magazine* in 2013 about how she came to practice restorative justice. An alternative to criminal justice proceedings, restorative justice aims to rehabilitate offenders and help them to make amends to their victims by allowing victims to participate more fully in the process.

Sexually abused by her father when she was a child, Baliga decided early on to channel the outrage and anger born from her trauma into becoming a lawyer so that she could lock up bad guys like her own father. Yet on a trip to Dharamsala, India, she met Tibetan exiles who recounted tragic stories of what they experienced when they fled the invading Chinese army. "Women getting raped, children made to kill their parents—unbelievably awful stuff," she remembered. She asked them, "How are you even standing, let alone smiling?" and they always answered, "Forgiveness."

Baliga was flummoxed by those who had experienced worse pain and suffering than she but who had found ways to move forward, peacefully. Upon advice, while in India, she wrote to the Dalai Lama asking for help on how to deal with her anger, the emotion that had served as her motivating force for so long. She didn't know how to work for the oppressed and abused without it. She was invited to speak with him, and he gave her this advice: to meditate alone, first, and then to align herself with her enemies. He asked her to open her heart to them. In response, Baliga said, she "laughed out loud."[12]

Later, through the meditation that the Dalai Lama recommended, Baliga did find forgiveness for her father. Then, she experienced a moment she describes as "complete relinquishment of anger, hatred and the desire for retribution and revenge." Baliga left her punishing days behind and started practicing restorative justice. She was one of the first to use the process in a homicide case.

Humans have a history of overcoming their differences, of improving themselves and finding creative ways to deal with conflict, violence, oppression, and trauma.

Could the same be true for abortion?

Moral Jujitsu

Journalist Emily Bazelon brought national awareness to the subject of postabortion counseling in her 2007 *New York Times Magazine* cover story "Is There a Post-Abortion Syndrome?" Her article showed how the political conflict over abortion had an impact on the way both sides addressed the topic. She wrote, "Anti-abortion advocates exaggerate the mental-health risks of abortion [and] some abortion advocates play down the emotional aftereffects." Conflicting ideologies determined each side's approach.

Even though the pro life activists worried about abortion's emotional aftermath, they weren't trying to prevent unwanted pregnancies or to help women support their babies. Instead, they focused on restricting and banning the procedure. In response to the "abortion hurts women" message, many pro-choice activists tried to explain away difficult feelings, attributing them to other underlying issues taking place in the lives of women. One activist, Ava Torre-Bueno, author of the book *Peace After Abortion*, admitted, "The last thing pro-choice people, myself included, want to do is to give people who want to make abortions harder to get or illegal one iota of help."[13] The public conversation about abortion emotions had finally begun.

Just three months after Bazelon's article was published, Exhale launched a series of postabortion e-cards. Within a day, the Associated Press published an article about our "Hallmark cards for abortion," and Rush Limbaugh took me to task on his radio show: "Now, this Baker babe, founder and executive director of Exhale [exhaling] said that she was 'unaware of anybody else providing after-abortion sympathy cards online.' How convoluted is this? If you're going to send a sympathy card to anybody after an abortion, shouldn't it be the aborted fetus?"[14]

By the time the week was over, I had done more than 20 radio and TV interviews, the majority of which were on conservative talk radio shows, including an hour live with the nationally syndicated Michael Medved and an appearance on Fox News with Martha MacCallum, where I debated the vice president of the Family Research Council.

Controversy erupted.

Carol Lloyd, a writer at Salon, practically patted my colleagues and me on the head, commenting, "The women at Exhale couldn't have known what they were getting themselves into. Antiabortionist bloggers are having a field day."[15] On CNN's *Paula Zahn Now*, pundits questioned whether the whole thing was a publicity stunt, though Roland Martin was forced to acknowledge that the faith-based e-card we offered—"The promise of God is to be with us through all of life's transitions. God will never leave you or forsake you. May you find comfort in God's constant love. Know that my prayers are with you at this time"—was biblically sound. Prolife blogs expressed confusion and dismay over our different messages, incredulous that our selection of e-cards had messages to address both grief and encouragement.

What, everyone seemed to wonder, were the women of Exhale thinking?

Since the launch of the talkline four years earlier, Exhale counselors had heard men and other loved ones express how difficult it was to find the right words to express their love and care to someone who had had an abortion. It was

clear that even if people didn't agree with an abortion decision, they were still interested in showing a loved one that
they cared. They just needed a little direction. As volunteers
kept taking these calls, we started to think about how Exhale
could help these significant others find the right words.

We wanted to find a culturally relevant way to help significant others show their loved ones who had had an abortion that they cared for them.

Hallmark. Greeting cards. We use cards in times of grief
and loss and in times of celebration and joy. There is literally a greeting card for everything from divorce to TGIF.
Exhale couldn't possibly afford or manage designing and
selling individual printed greeting cards, but what could we
do on the Internet?

On March 13, 2007, we launched six different postabortion e-cards on our website with messages about grief and
loss, encouragement and support, including the infamous
faith based message for Christian and Catholic women who
have had abortions.

The hate mail came quickly, instigated by Limbaugh. The
phones rang off the hook with media requests, mostly from
conservative outlets. My coworkers and I felt attacked, under
siege. We wanted to defend ourselves, to fight back, to come
out swinging. And yet, we knew that we had the rare chance
to try something different, to resist getting sucked into the
same old us-versus-them abortion battle. Our team made a
choice: we would approach every hater and every attack with
unconditional love and compassion.

We compiled a list of behaviors for ourselves, and we
wrote them in big letters on a piece of flip-chart paper and

posted it to the wall: Empathy. Love. Compassion. We committed ourselves to treating respectfully those who attacked and threatened us.

I released the anger that I felt toward Rush Limbaugh and his listeners who flooded our inbox with their vitriol. I saw them as the distractions they were, attempts to force Exhale to join the fight, to act with hostility instead of empathy. I chose to keep listening. I let go of the need to defend myself or Exhale. Instead, I used every media opportunity to reach out beyond the attackers and speak directly to the audience, letting them know that Exhale was a place of comfort and care. My message would never have come through as genuine if I had come off as outraged, defensive, or bitter.

The only way to promote compassion was to practice it, fearlessly and publicly.

Over 5,000 e-cards were sent that week alone. Today, other organizations make their own e-cards for a range of stigmatized identities and events, from abortion to the celebration of queer and poor families and single moms. Pro-voice utilizes cultural tools to generate respect for marginalized experiences, promoting individual and community health and wellbeing while shifting social norms to greater acceptance.

Leading the Way

Now women and men can access more connection and support after an abortion than ever before. Both sides have evolved their approaches considerably since Bazelon's investigation, embracing more emotional nuances and accepting a broader range of strategies to promote postabortion health and wellbeing.

Independent pro-life organizations have sprung up to meet the needs of women who aren't religious, including Abortion Changes You, a website that launched in 2010 with a founding story that sounded remarkably similar to Exhale's (the founder reached out to many of the journalists who covered Exhale's talkline launch, claiming to be "like Exhale," with a personal story very like my own). The site suggests a variety of healing pathways to address the impact of abortion, saying, "Each person will go through the process differently."[16] Additionally, the site notes, "Many people find it helpful to start by telling their stories and building their support systems."[17]

The new organization indicated a shift in the pro-life approach to women's emotions and experiences. Judgmental labels like "postabortive women" and "postabortion syndrome" and phrases like "abortion's aftermath" became less common. A new pro-life focus on healing from grief and loss, rather than seeking forgiveness for a sin, emerged.

Meanwhile, the pro-choice side raced to catch up.

Planned Parenthood updated their counseling methods. In 2007, I advised them about a brand-new mandatory staff-training program on how to address patient emotions after an abortion. This training came with explicit directions to refer clients and patients to Exhale as well as other newly available local and national emotional-support resources.

In 2004, a couple of years after Exhale's talkline launched, Grayson Dempsey launched Backline out of Portland, Oregon. A national pregnancy options talkline, Backline was one of the first pro-choice groups to advertise the availability of its postabortion counseling services. Then came Faith Aloud out of Missouri, formerly a chapter of the Religious Coalition for Reproductive Choice, started by Reverend Rebecca Turner, whose clergy-staff line expanded nationally in 2008. Connect & Breathe, an effort of the Unitarian Universalist church of Rochester, New York, was inspired by the abortion experience of its church leader, Reverend Kaaren Anderson. In 2011, they launched a talkline service to carry out their church's mission of "creating connection by listening to our deepest selves, opening to life's gifts, and serving needs greater than our own."

In addition to the new national talklines, a number of regional services were started, including Emerge, out of Minneapolis, Minnesota, a project of Pro-Choice Resources. Emerge is a discussion support group for women who have had abortions. Although Emerge is staffed by a pro-choice agency, the women who attend come from all backgrounds, including many who are pro-life. Emerge is one of the few in-person, local services that have been able to survive over a long period of time. (Often, efforts spawned by one person's dedication and interest—a physician, a therapist, a yoga instructor, or a New Age spiritualist—are short-lived. Maintaining these programs solo is tough, especially over the long term.)

That's not all. In 2007, two women from New York City— Mary Mahoney and Lauren Mitchell—had the idea of applying the concept of a birth doula to abortion. Traditionally, doulas provide emotional support and care to a person going through birth. When the Doula Project began offering abortion doula support services within Planned Parenthood clinics, a new national movement was launched. Now, there are abortion doula projects—more accurately called "full spectrum" doulas—across the country, supporting people throughout their pregnancy experiences. The groups have been particularly cognizant of developing care models for transgender and gay families, but they continue to face obstacles getting inside abortion clinics. The movement is primarily run and operated by volunteers.

Exhale disrupted conventional thinking about postabortion support, and organizations and advocates adapted. The pro-life side toned down their harsh judgments and created room for a broader range of feelings and outcomes, and the pro-choice side developed new counseling protocols and referral practices in their clinics. All over the country, new organizations and services sprang up to meet women's emotional needs around their abortions, led primarily by a new kind of "conscious constituent." Like the activists who drove the repeal movement of the 1960s, these new abortion well-being advocates were often driven to service through their connections to women having abortions. It is still rare to see the people who need these services start them.

The changes that have taken place in the last decade are a giant step in the right direction, but the growing field of postabortion support remains political as well as divided. What's needed next is for pro-voice practitioners from all sides to take the leap to work across their political differences toward a broader culture of respect and empathy. This comes with significant political risk for activists, yet pro-voice offers a framework that gives advocates purpose for stepping outside the safe parameters of their group.

When my cofounders launched Exhale without picking a side, we did so knowing:

1. that *pro-choice* was a conservative term, designed to appeal to antigovernment libertarians who didn't like the government involved in their guns or their bedrooms;[18]

2. that the violence and intimidating tactics of the pro-life movement were scary and intimidating to women who had walked through crowds of unsympathetic protestors on their way to clinics to get an abortion; and

3. that most Americans identify as both pro-choice and pro-life, symbolizing the public's ability to embrace nuanced realities.[19]

These observations led my cofounders and me to believe that there was an opening to try something different, to address a hunger for change. We assumed that the criticism directed at us would give way to invention, sparking new ways to talk and think about abortion that were better suited to match Americans in their nuanced views and women in their personal experiences. We were right. The conversation has changed significantly, but it took years of more criticism before we saw former skeptics adopt our ideas as their own.

The process to expand the cultural conversation over abortion has not been easy. Initially, the demands of the conflict far outweighed the desire for any change in tactics or strategy. As much as the terms *pro-choice* and *pro-life* were insufficient, they were still the only way to decipher who was on your side; and in the midst of war, knowing who is friend or foe is far better than sailing into uncharted political waters.

I'll never forget the time during Exhale's early years when a few of our most vocal pro-choice critics sat beside us in a national meeting for women's health leaders, lamenting the narrowness of the pro-choice frame and its labels, referencing the critiques made by women of color and their desire to have more options. The next day, these same leaders waged new attacks against us, organizing their allies to be suspicious of our motives and to withdraw their support because we wouldn't adhere to pro-choice doctrine.

There was no way to win. And it wasn't just Exhale that was losing.

It was the beginning of the new millennium, and the abortion conflict itself seemed unwinnable. Stuck. If risk and innovation were rejected, then sticking together was rewarded. Being on the correct side of the conflict had become far more important than making significant cultural change.

As confusing, hurtful, and frustrating as that time was for my cofounders and me, it was also revealing. It showed that Exhale had a lot more to offer the world than just counseling after an abortion. We saw the opportunity in the obstacle. We understood that if everyone else was afraid of what happened in the spaces between black and white, between us versus them, and between pro-choice and pro-life, then we could develop our strengths in the place everyone avoided: the gray area. We made it our home.

The *gray area* is not the mushy middle of the political poles or a place in which to forge common ground between those who typically disagree. The gray area is the chaotic result of our social, technological, demographic, and political evolution. It is the layered, complicated web that makes up our true lives. It is the regret after a choice rightly made, the benefits of having less worldwide physical violence alongside increases in domestic structural inequity. Our efforts to make technology cheap and easy to use, to end discrimination and increase our rights, and to connect the dots between what ails our communities and our environment have produced an entirely new set of challenges for how we live together, peacefully.

"The gray area," international pop superstar Justin Timberlake once explained, "the place between black and white. That's the place where life happens. The gray area is where you become an adult."[20] The opportunities of the gray area are many, whether you're a maturing adolescent, an aspiring entrepreneur, or a peace activist in the nation's abortion conflict. Within the gray areas are the possibilities to shape what happens next, given the fresh insights and lived experiences that come from new realities.

My Exhale cofounders and I made up our own label. We were pro-voice.

At its core, pro-voice is about giving the world what it needs most. It's about creating a compassionate vision for change that encompasses the needs of your allies along with those of your enemies. It means caring about those who are different from you, whether in racial background or in worldview. It's about forming connection in place of division, listening instead of shouting, respecting instead of judging. It's a discipline for innovators and creators who, when they spot a problem or need, see a challenge. Instead of working to destroy what's broken, pro-voice people build, create, innovate, and improve.

Exhale never adopted the pro-choice position. In fact, the opposite happened. In 2013, Planned Parenthood dropped the labels, recognizing their inability to connect with Americans who have layered views about abortion. They publicly embraced gray areas. One Planned Parenthood ad posted online on January 10, 2013, demonstrated their new approach. It read, "[T]he labels of being pro-choice and pro-life are not so cut and dry. There is a lot of gray area for people who classify themselves in either category."

Planned Parenthood's decision was not a retreat but a reflection of the times. Clear-cut battles of good versus evil and right versus wrong are hard to find. Racism still exists despite the US electing a black president. Sexism exists despite Sheryl Sandberg. With a closer look after the 2012 elections, technology showed us that the United States isn't so much a nation of red and blue states as it is various shades of purple. Almost half of Americans define themselves as both "pro-choice" and "pro-life."[21] America lives in the gray areas, presenting a host of exciting challenges and opportunities that are ripe for creative innovation.

Exhale was ahead of its time. While many factors contributed to Planned Parenthood's decision to shift their approach, Exhale's founding board president, Lisa Lepson, commented on the unique role that Exhale played in the evolution of the public abortion conversation in the *Stanford Social Innovation Review*:

What social entrepreneurs do for social change is unique. They arrive on the scene, bring attention to community needs previously ignored, push the envelope, raise questions, and provide an alternative view and voice. They tackle problems with innovative models and impact large-scale public perceptions. Often, they work in fields dominated by large, established organizations with complicated networks of stakeholders and bureaucratic systems with large budgets. But these established organizations aren't often nimble, and they struggle to adapt to contemporary needs. So when an organization such as Planned Parenthood . . . makes a major change and begins to own progressive messaging and values, it is years in the making.

That's how a social entrepreneur can measure their impact. Years after their radical idea is rejected by mainstream organizations, the very same organizations will adopt them and promote these ideas as their own. Success for the social entrepreneur happens when their views are no longer feared but embraced.[22]

When Exhale left the black-and-white debate behind and ventured toward the gray areas of real life, we made it our mission to do what everyone else was afraid to try. We started experimenting and testing practices that could lead to a world beyond the conflict.

In her *SSIR* piece, Lepson noted what happened when I put forward my radical viewpoint, suggesting that the political labels of pro-choice and pro-life got in the way of our mission and advocating that we should leave the labels behind:

You can imagine the response we got at the time. Established organizations working in the field of abortion rights were dumbfounded, threatened, confused, and angry. We were told to pick a side or "admit" that we were pro-choice. We faced suspicion and outright hostility. It didn't matter how we tried to explain it. No one got it yet. It was a novel, daring approach, and Exhale's board, staff, and volunteers spent the next decade advocating our view.[23]

Along the way, I got a lot of horrible advice. The hardest to take came from those who wanted to help Exhale succeed, and to help me, in particular, as a young leader. Unfortunately, their idea of success was often predicated on my letting my naïve notions of another way go and accepting that, to be anything substantial, we'd have to be pro-choice. "The only way to get money," one leader said, "is for Exhale to be pro-choice, because that's where the money is."

Her advice was a perfect "aha" moment. The choice between being mission based and being money based was clear. In our first few years, when funding was nonexistent and our purpose mistrusted, Exhale was promised some level of short-term success if I chose to pursue pro-choice money to fund the organization that was putting me into personal debt, but I also understood that it would be a strategic decision to abandon our core mission.

It was a dilemma I faced early. This was the single most defining moment of my leadership, because the result shaped my future decisions and led to more hard calls. I chose the mission.

I decided that whether or not Exhale ever raised another dollar, I needed to do work that was a mission match, work that I believed in. Even if Exhale was only ever a small group of volunteers working freely on a local effort, I still believed that the time and energy we spent practicing abortion peace would be, in the long term, more significant for social change than any bigger, well-funded, politically motivated, and ideologically identified organization could accomplish.

Choosing mission was the bigger risk for me. It had the least likelihood of success. It was also what mattered most to me. I believed in a world beyond the conflict, and I couldn't fathom investing anything—my time, energy, or emotion—into helping the conflict grow.

I thought that someone, some organization, somehow, at some time was going to have to be the one to withstand the pressure to pick a side and be willing to take the hits that come with going another route. It might as well be us. What did we have to lose?

Plenty, it turns out. Exhale lost board members. We lost volunteers. We lost donors. We lost friends and allies who thought that if they could just explain the facts of the political matter, we'd see the light and join them in the fight. It wasn't that we didn't understand what was at stake in the debate. It was that we weren't in the political fight.

We had a lot to gain, too. The very innovation that turned off so many people was what drew many to Exhale. We weren't going to be the place that people would come to get better at fighting; instead, we'd be the place that people would come to get better at listening, resolving, creating, and innovating. We'd be the place that everyone longed for but didn't know existed. We'd be the place of hope and possibility, support and respect, rather than anger and outrage, judgment and attack.

For years, when I was interviewed by journalists, wrote blog posts, or appeared on TV, my words fell into an abyss. I believed there were people listening who wanted to hear what I had to say, who had been waiting for someone to say it. I didn't know what they looked like or where they came from, but I had faith that my people were out there and they were waiting. If I wasn't fully myself, if I didn't speak the truth as I lived it or share the vision I held closely in my heart, they would never know we were the same. The only way for us to find each other was for me to say what I experienced and what I believed, even though it seemed so impossible and radically different from any other voice at the time.

It worked.

People responded to the message. We found each other. There are people and funders who get excited about innovation, even if it scares the heck out of them. And the more Exhale was public and vocal about what we were trying to do, the more we found people who were ready to be a part of something new and challenging. We learned that people working deep inside bureaucracies needed Exhale to help them push for changes they had long wanted to make in their own organizations but couldn't implement alone. We found journalists who were sick and tired of conflict reporting and who were poised to bring a fresh perspective forward. We inspired new champions and empowered change makers to take risks that have led to many of the cultural changes we can now witness. If before Exhale had tried to make ourselves a safe bet, now we were upfront about how little we could promise. We were direct about what we knew, what we hoped to learn, and what we weren't sure would work. All of a sudden, program officers at major foundations were proudly claiming us as a "risky grant." Our funding wasn't stable or significant, but it existed.

Outside the organization, many people thought we were lying about our true position, were hiding it, or were just gutless. Who could blame them? There had never been a third way on abortion. Some had tried to find one—whether it was the pro-choice turn to the right; the pro-life turn to a message about women's wellbeing; or the organization called Third Way, which was founded in Washington, DC in 2005 to help pro-life Democrats get elected in conservative areas. These alternative approaches to the conflict generally involved a sacrifice of critically important values and beliefs. It was hard to see how a new approach to abortion could be sustained. Or why it should be.

Exhale was living in a space that no one else wanted to acknowledge. What would happen, many long-term abortion activists wondered, if there was public acknowledgment that a woman needed emotional support after an abortion? Didn't support for abortion rights require people to think the procedure was no big deal? Or, on the flip side, didn't our desire to support women's emotions after abortion demand that we recognize that abortion was harmful and therefore wrong, warranting us to take a political stand against it?

It was difficult for anyone to grasp what possible benefit a nonpartisan approach to abortion could have for women, democracy, or social change.

Pro-Voice Television

When I received the e-mail from MTV casting looking for help to find women to go on a television special to talk about their abortions, Exhale had already spent a few years exploring the opportunities and challenges of abortion storytelling. I sent a short response, detailing a few suggestions that would help make the show relevant to their audience and supportive of the storytellers. Within hours of hitting "Send," I received a phone call from one of the producers.

The abortion special, *No Easy Decision*, was taking place because one of the cast members from the widely popular and controversial show *16 & Pregnant*—Markai Durham—had gotten pregnant again. She had invited a film crew to follow her and her family as they went through the abortion together. MTV wanted to make a special out of her experience, but they didn't want to show Markai as the only woman having an abortion. They were recruiting others to join the special so that Markai didn't look so alone.

Over the next few weeks, I talked to the producer several times about her approach, scripting, and message, and I shared insights and lessons learned from our experiences. We weren't the only ones working behind the scenes. The National Campaign to Prevent Teen and Unplanned Pregnancy had a long working relationship with MTV, and their entertainment staff had given Exhale a thumbs-up to the producer. I was skeptical of MTV and the final product, yet I wanted to advocate for the women who had had abortions whom I knew would be members of the audience watching this special.

I wanted to make sure that the women in their audience who had had abortions felt less alone and more supported and respected as a result of the special.

As these calls with the producer continued, Exhale started to hatch our own plan. Given everything we knew about what happens to women who share their stories publicly, we were greatly concerned about how the young women might be politicized, judged, and dragged into the center of the abortion battle. We knew these women were gutsy and willing to take big risks, but we also didn't want the women appearing on the show to be left hanging.

We wanted to send them a message: We're with you. We have your back.

We had just received some funding from the Ford Foundation, and for the very first time in Exhale's history, we had some cash with which to get creative. We got to work. We created an online campaign called "16 & Loved," a riff off of 16 & Pregnant, which had the singular goal of generating love for the three women—Markai Durham, Katie Stack, and Natalia Koss Vallejo—who would appear on the show.[24] That was the sole purpose.

Exhale planned to ignore everything else that had the potential to distract us from our goal—such as criticizing MTV; or Dr. Drew, who was hosting the special; or especially the politics of abortion—and keep our eyes on the prize: supporting the courageous women sharing their stories. We would organize people online to make sure these women didn't launch themselves into abortion history at the mercy of the polarizing media.

"16 & Loved" was a campaign with a number of components, including the creation of a website where anyone could post a message of support and love, as long as it was free of politics and judgment. We didn't allow people to make sweeping assumptions about what women who have abortions feel, nor use their stories to make a political point—i.e., draw a final moral conclusion. Other components included live-blogging of the television event by prominent feminist leaders and community building on Facebook and Twitter.

There was significant skepticism about whether or not it was useful to run a campaign without a political bent. Many didn't think it was possible. There was a lot of interest in using the special to slam MTV for their past sins, and Dr. Drew in particular, who had built up a reputation for his judgmental attitude toward his guests. We were warned not to work with MTV, that the exploitative network was no friend of women and certainly not of feminism, and that we'd get duped, played for a fool.

There was safety in sitting in the wings, critiquing MTV from a distance, but we were seeking to influence and shape the product. We wanted to make pro-voice television.

Exhale's reputation was on the line with many prominent public thought leaders, especially those who were skeptical of our pro-voice approach. We could earn some new believers if the show was good, but if the show was a disaster, we'd lose credibility. My relationship with the producer was a new one, and there was no reason for me to trust what she said or that she'd take any of my advice. I gave it anyway.

Exhale had another dilemma. MTV had made it perfectly clear that everyone involved with the show was under strict embargo. We were not supposed to talk about it publicly. MTV was planning to air the show late at night, between

Christmas and New Year's, with no promotion and no planned repeats. It was a one-shot deal. By that time, we also knew that Exhale would be featured as a primary resource on the show. Dr. Drew would refer the audience to our national talkline, the number would flash across the screen, and we'd be featured on the website. We did not want to mess this up.

We continued our behind-the-scenes organizing to prepare for the launch of "16 & Loved" while keeping our fingers crossed that none of the bloggers we were talking to would get itchy to spill the beans before it was time. We needed to respect the wishes of MTV and do our part to make sure that the special had as much impact as possible for our community. It was exciting to be a part of something so trendsetting and revolutionary.

In the final days before the premiere, the producer flew from New York City to Oakland to show the Exhale community one of the final versions of the special and invite our feedback. Exhale staff members and volunteer counselors, along with a few key supporters, gathered together to watch the episode. It was breathtaking. We were all mesmerized by the chance to see what we'd heard on our talkline for so many years come alive on the screen. We loved how the special showed Markai with her boyfriend and family dealing with the decision together, and we were smitten with Katie and Natalia. At one point, the three women were sitting side by side on the couch, Natalia between Katie and Markai, when Natalia reached out instinctively and grabbed both of their hands. It was a poignant emotional moment, and the image they projected simply by holding hands—of connection, solidarity, support, and understanding—was a wonder to behold.

The following day, an Exhale volunteer who had been present for the screening sent me an e-mail mentioning an element of the special that she found particularly judgmental. It was a comment made by Dr. Drew that struck us all as a bit unwarranted. I passed that e-mail along to the producer, not expecting or knowing if any changes could be made at that point. The same day, I had a conference call with many of the bloggers who we hoped would participate in our campaign, some of whom were regular critics of Dr. Drew. I had to acknowledge that they would probably find some fault with his approach but that overall it was a terrific show and we hoped they'd stay focused on the women.

Our need to start promoting the show without violating the embargo was answered by *Entertainment Weekly*, which let the news of the pending special slip in a blog article online. It was go time!

The supportive messages started to trickle into our campaign website. In the beginning, people didn't quite know how to be loving and respectful without making it political, but with a few tips, it started to click. We had just a few days to generate comments before the show aired, and we later learned that Markai, Natalia, and Katie—and their entire families—were reading every single post. They texted each other and made sure that they had seen the latest submission. Their families, inspired by the bravery of their daughters and sisters, had been worried about how they might be treated by the public and the media. Our site, showing love to three women whom America had yet to meet, gave their families confidence and hope that it would turn out OK. They were all feeling the love.

When *No Easy Decision* finally aired, all the concerns, skepticism, and fear about what message the show would convey faded away.[25] The final special was amazing. Seriously. I had never seen a better example of pro-voice come alive. It was honest, complex, emotional, and powerful, and there wasn't a single judgment or mention of politics to tarnish the realities of the human experience of abortion.

In addition to the messages of love and support that our campaign website received, we got something we hadn't asked for: personal stories. Women were sharing, and not just young women, the regular audience of MTV. Women of all ages, including those who had had abortions years ago, found something special and needed in *No Easy Decision*.

Here's a sample of the more than 240 messages:

Angie wrote:

> To Markai, Natalia and Katie. You are all so very courageous to come on national TV and tell your story. I was 19 when I made the decision and I knew that if I had to live with roommates to be on my own, I sure as heck couldn't raise a child effectively. I did have the support of my family and was able to turn to them in my time of need, but I rarely tell anyone else about the decision I made all these years ago. My biggest reason for having an abortion was that I didn't want to end up on Oprah in 20 or 30 years asking if my child forgave me and had a good life. I couldn't be stuck wondering what happened to them. I did have complications after the procedure and with all the cramping and pain I was having, the clinic thought I might need an additional

D&C. Eventually everything turned out ok and I recovered. I was awake for mine and the only thing they gave me was numbing medicine and laughing gas. By the time it was all over I was laughing because I couldn't get my pants on and crying because I was alone. It is ok to grieve, cry, and be sad. But don't hold it in to the point that it is harming your mental well being. After 10 years I am ok with my decision and maybe I will have kids one day, but right now I know that it was the right thing to do.

Keep your head up.

Jess wrote:

I had an abortion at age twenty because I didn't want to have a baby I couldn't take care of, financially or emotionally. I was physically and mentally fragile and very, very ill, so there was no way I could've continued my pregnancy.

I'm very proud of all of you for being so responsible and thoughtful and I want you to know that there are millions of women just like you who have struggled with these issues. You are not alone and you are loved.

Kathryn wrote:

I am a huge advocate for women's reproductive rights and have been for a long time. I have family and friends that feel the same way and yet, when I became unexpectedly pregnant I found it nearly impossible to talk to a single soul. The conversation of abortion is so stigmatized and concealed I felt scared to open up to people I knew would love and support me unconditionally anyway. Even when I was able to confide in my best friend, there was a void in her support, because she could not possibly relate to what I was going through, but I had no one to turn to that could. By appearing on "No Easy Decision," you've filled that void; and though my decision was made long ago, there are girls out there who will face similar choices and you will be there for them. We are now connected in the most intimate of female experience and I am now here for you as you are for me; so thank you so very much. My deepest and most sincere appreciation goes out to you.

49 wrote:

as I watched the show unfold (very well done too), I worried about the backlash you would surely endure. I thought what brave young women you all are, and wanted to seek out a place to send you a supportive message. I was so happy to find this site!

I am 49, have had an abortion in my past. it was the best thing I could do for my family at the time, and I have no regrets. I do not revisit it very often. for sure it is still there under the surface, but does not interfere with my daily life in any way!

it was not an easy decision then, and would not be an easy decision today. had I a chance to do it over again with the same set of circumstances, I would have chosen the same procedure.

my advice, do not let this define who you are. and, know that you are loved!

Markai, please tell your Mother that I send her my best wishes, and that she is a wonderful example of unconditional love!

S wrote:

I just want to thank everyone involved with this. I had an abortion a few months ago and I have been having a hard time dealing with it. The holidays made me extremely sad and I have been having a difficult time coping. But tonight's show opened my eyes and my heart. I can honestly say that I don't feel so alone now and I can finally heal. Thank you so much for doing this. The girls are my heroes and I felt so connected to them. You're in my heart.

Denise wrote:

It's always nice to hear stories and know you're not alone. This episode has helped me a lot. Although I am not fully 'okay' with the decision I made, I have to learn everyday how to cope with it. I wish to someday be able to speak about it as well as these brave women! Thank you ladies!

The "16 & Loved" website was a politics-free site that wasn't asking for stories, but women brought and shared their stories because they had been invited to participate in a community of mutual love and support. They knew that every submission and comment was moderated, that it was protected and wouldn't be turned into a shouting match. Under the right conditions, women were ready and wanted to connect with each other in personal ways.

And the concerns that one Exhale volunteer talkline counselor had shared about some of Dr. Drew's comments? Those remarks were gone. Edited out. Dr. Drew came off like a teddy bear—warm, fuzzy, and kind. Jamia Wilson, blogging for the Women's Media Center, wrote that given "what I have witnessed when watching Dr. Drew on '16 and Pregnant' and 'Teen Mom' reunion specials, it was astonishing to see that Dr. Drew's deferential and nonjudgmental treatment of abortion and his sympathetic interactions with the women on the show drastically differed from his past conduct on MTV."[26]

Thanks to our "16 & Loved" campaign, the special generated a lot more press than it would have on its own, given its late-night, one-time showing. The articles the next day had such titles as "MTV's Shockingly Good Abortion Special," "MTV's Abortion Show Was . . . Actually Good," "MTV's Abortion Special Treats Issue with Compassion and Facts," "Love for the Women of MTV's No Easy Decision," and "MTV Abortion Special 'No Easy Decision' Treats Abortion with Compassionate Integrity." There wasn't a single article about *No Easy Decision* that didn't mention "16 & Loved."

Exhale's campaign had worked. We had successfully driven the public conversation about the special away from the polarizing politics of the day and toward a conversation about how to give love and support to women who had had abortions. We had never been more confident about the social impact of the pro-voice discipline.

It got even better. Feminist Jessica Valenti spoke for many when she acknowledged that the special was "a pleasant surprise."[27]

It wasn't just feminists who thought MTV had done a good job. At first glance, Fox News conservative commentator Bill O'Reilly assumed that the special was glorifying abortion, but his own cultural warriors—Gretchen Carlson, a Fox News morning show anchor, and Margaret Hoover, a conservative political strategist—agreed that the program was "compelling and neutral." "It was not a cavalier decision she made," Carlson said of Markai Durham. "I actually felt that this might deter young people from having abortions."[28] O'Reilly was forced to admit that he "might be wrong" about the way he thought abortion should be presented in the media.

Neither Valenti nor O'Reilly would ever be accused of representing the mushy middle of American politics, but the fact that each of these cultural trendsetters responded in a positive way and that both conservatives and liberals found something compelling about the program points toward new possibilities for a pro-voice public discourse.

When abortion is approached in a complex, emotional manner and when personal stories illuminate gray areas, there is something for everyone. People on opposing sides of the issue can find meaning in the conversation, and those who share the experience can find a way to relate. When abortion conversations are grounded in the level of nuanced, complicated personal experience, there is a unique opportunity to talk about abortion in a civil, respectful way, something our culture desperately needs to witness and practice.

Entertainment Weekly confirmed the value of an emotional approach to abortion in the media. When an episode of *Friday Night Lights* that included the story of a character having an abortion did not generate any controversy, *EW* noted that there is very little uproar when a TV series addresses abortion with "emotional honesty and nuance."[29]

This is why pro-voice advocates listen instead of fight.

When Exhale built something that actual people needed— like the e-cards and "16 & Loved"—we could drive a new conversation rather than respond to one. We could act rather than react. When it was all said and done, the *New York Times* put Exhale on the home page of their website in an article detailing our efforts to be pro-voice in an ever-polarized pro-choice and pro-life world. We created news, too.

We didn't do it by fighting. We did it because Markai, Katie, and Natalia—and their families—needed to know that they were loved despite whatever judgment and attacks might come their way. Our "16 & Loved" campaign helped meet that need. Publicly advocating love in a judgmental culture shifted the conversation away from the typical us-versus-them terms of the political conflict and toward everyone's role in loving and caring for the women in our lives who have abortions.

Our culture got unstuck on abortion, even if just for a moment. If it happened once, it can happen again.

Abortion Peace

From Exhale's earliest work listening to the women and men who called the after-abortion talkline, we learned that personal stories about abortion were richer and more varied than either existing political frame encompassed. We discovered that what people felt, did, and needed went well beyond the limited stories showcased in the public sphere.

We created pro-voice to reflect those feelings and meet those needs.

Unlike many well-known negotiation frameworks for conflict resolution that seek to bring opposing sides together to play nice and form agreements and compromises, pro-voice is founded on a complete dedication to transformation. The difference between the two approaches—between resolution and transformation—lies in the idea that peace is possible in the present, not a theoretical future. Our commitment is to expand the capacity for creative thinking and thus open possibilities for innovation. Our belief is that a transformative approach can, according to peace expert Eyal Rabinovitch, lead to "wiser answers to common struggles and to the creation of stronger societies able to maintain integrity in public life even through profound differences."[30]

Peace in this perspective isn't a world without fighting or conflict but rather it's one where conflict can be engaged in—fiercely and directly—without dehumanizing ourselves or our opponents. Staying above the fray, so to speak, we will know how peaceful we are, not by whether we stop disagreeing but in how we respond to each other when we do.

A significant portion of this book has been spent exploring how Exhale opened up ways of thinking even though abortion was locked in polarity. Sparking curiosity and enabling discovery are hallmarks of pro-voice practice. Personal stories are the missing link, the game changer, for shedding new light on stuck issues, but not for the reasons many people assume. It is not the emotionally manipulative or persuasive power of stories that pro-voice seeks to harness for a predetermined solution, but rather the complexity of gray areas that is their most powerful strength. When used to open conversations, stories invite listeners to imagine themselves in someone else's shoes, to ponder alternative scenarios and solutions previously unimagined. It's this engagement inside the story that makes creative thinking possible.

Being pro-voice and following its philosophy is a much different type of duty than checking a box on your ballot, placing a bumper sticker on your car, marching in a protest, or retweeting a hashtag, though certainly it can include all of those things. To be pro-voice is to practice a set of behaviors, a way of being in the world. It requires practitioners who engage in conflicted issues like abortion to let black-and-white answers go in order to create space for more gray areas. Illustrating complexity through hidden stories or using words that have multiple meanings eliminates the wink-wink of political jargon so often used to signal an allegiance to one side or the other, letting a group know which side you're on. What happens at a party when the president's position on abortion comes up, and everyone else starts their sentences with "Well, I'm pro-life, so . . ." or "Of course, I'm pro-choice, and . . . ," and you offer no label, no way to identify where you might fall on the spectrum? This is where the rubber meets the road of culture change. It's one thing to believe in the power of connection over division; it's quite another to stand in the gray areas while everyone around you claims to be black or white.

If we really want to move the nation and the culture beyond the divisiveness and dehumanizing impact of the abortion wars, actions like these have to become more commonplace. It isn't a game. Refusing to pick a label or "hint" at your true stance isn't a sophisticated game of devil's advocate or an intellectual trick played to make someone else look foolish under your scrutinizing eye. It must be genuine, expressing vulnerability and displaying an authenticity that, as unnerving and unusual as it may be, is also compelling and intriguing for its novel approach.

It's a huge challenge to follow the pro-voice path, which is why it can't be achieved as a series of solo acts in private moments. Fundamental to the pro-voice philosophy is the value of collective action driven from shared lived experiences and the need to link individual behavior to larger social purposes. No one should be doing this unless there is a way to do it with others. Community building among similarly oriented allies is crucial to pro voice practice, too. Identifying champions and connecting them to one another through a global network of pro-voice advocates is a strategic approach to leveraging personal and local actions for broader, society-wide cultural change.

This network approach makes pro-voice especially important for the modern challenges and opportunities presented by life in the gray areas. The pro-voice model for peace looks more like our natural world—it's an ecosystem with overlapping networks that rely on each other for their health and vitality—than it does a human-made road leading toward justice. When the perfect peaceful world exists only in a far distant future, it's easy to ignore the opportunities for well-being that exist in the current moment. But when change makers learn how to identify the tangible, real-life examples of truth and justice in their own lives, they have the power to nurture the growth and expansion of these values.

Using the pro-voice model, we don't all have to be walking the same linear road to a utopian destination that we won't reach in our lifetime. Instead, we can build individual and social practices that cultivate our visions in our everyday lives, invite new participation, support fresh efforts, and work together to amplify our collective impact on a global scale.

Chapter 5

Shape What's Next

Pro-voice is everywhere. It lives all around us. Inspiring examples of the human desire to overcome differences and hostility with love and compassion happen all the time. By bringing existing pro-voice efforts to light and connecting the dots between pro-voice action and behavior, the pro-voice movement can grow far beyond the issue of abortion.

Here are just a few examples of where I witness pro-voice already taking place:

* I'm inspired by the work of Joan Blades and Mark Meckler to *rehumanize toxic dynamics* in politics. Blades, the founder of MoveOn, MomsRising, and Living Room Conversations, and well-known for her liberal passions, teamed up with Meckler, a Tea Party leader, to show in their joint appearances around the country that civil dialogue across the political aisle is possible.[1] They are serving as role models for how to disagree, often vehemently, about policy and priorities with respect for one another.

* When a video about street harassment went viral in 2014 (it was viewed more than 32 million times in one week), I was impressed by how feminist activists were concerned that only men of color were shown to be the culprits when they knew that men from all

backgrounds can harass women who are just walking down the street. The public conversation that took place about the video *affirmed and sustained the human dignity* of the men depicted in the video, whose sexist behavior was rightly criticized.

* Recognizing that the makeup of families in America is increasingly diverse, the Strong Families initiative of the reproductive-justice organization Forward Together employed the artistry of their multiracial community to *generate creativity and imagination* to recognize all types of families. Their Mama's Day e-cards celebrate the love of every kind of mama, from lesbian and single moms to poor moms and those in prison.

* I can't think of a bolder, more utopian and idealistic vision for humankind than the one espoused by the prison-abolition movement. It's hard to wrap my brain around the idea of a world without prisons, but I love the challenge it represents to consider more connecting, healing, empathetic—and effective—methods to address crime and right wrongs. Abolitionists *spur innovative thinking and action* with their radical goal.

* Black-and-white, us-versus-them binary thinking pervades so many aspects of how humans perceive our world, including the way we think about gender. But not everyone is comfortable checking a box marked "male" or "female." The growing movement for transgender rights and acceptance challenges traditional notions of what it means to be a woman or a man and *invites openness, engagement, and conversation* about gender identity, roles, and expression previously ignored.

Nothing is simple or easy about these examples. Each one is a challenge to the status quo and an attempt to create more social and cultural respect for what makes us different from one another—whether it's opposing political views, personal backgrounds and identities, or our social and cultural values. Most important, each example has real human stories hidden behind topics considered politically controversial. They represent a choice to love rather than hate, forgive rather than seek revenge, and listen rather than fight.

For example, ending street harassment won't be accomplished solely by calling out sexist oppression and bad male behavior. In the long term, women and men will have to work together to reimagine and renegotiate their relationships, as intimates and strangers. The new visibility of transgender people will further complicate—and by that I mean further—the conversation about what constitutes respectful engagement and behavior between people of all genders. In the case of political polarization, Blades and Meckler are refusing to take the easy route of turning their political opposition into caricatures and stereotypes, instead choosing to act civilly despite receiving criticism from their own sides.

For many, these examples of collaborating with the enemy, or in some cases the oppressor, to develop new social and cultural norms flies in the face of common sense and even human nature. And yet I am sincere when I say that pro-voice is antisacrifice.

This may come as a surprise to many readers. The biggest misconception I hear about pro-voice is that it requires people to sacrifice their beliefs—especially deeply held political ones. I hear the concern that to be pro-voice is to give away something dear, special, and important, and to let the hated and hateful "other side" win. Worst of all, I hear the concern that being pro-voice means having to accept being hurt yet again by those who have already caused pain, this time having to swallow it instead of fighting back.

Nothing could be further from the truth of what it means to be pro-voice. Pro-voice is a movement built on our individual and collective strengths, driven by creativity and innovation, and fueled by a shared commitment to wellbeing and peace. Pro-voice is a discipline, and its philosophy and tools are designed to support and enable—not abandon—its practitioners by helping them to honor what is most sacred to them.

I can't say it strongly enough: pro-voice should help you feel energized, empowered, and excited for what's next. It's the antithesis of burnout, exhaustion, and overwhelm. The power and influence of pro-voice is measured, in part, by the happiness of those who practice it. Cultivating happiness is fundamental to pro-voice because we need to be able to walk into conflict with a full heart capable of seeing the humanity in our enemy, a challenge that becomes nearly impossible if we are sick from exhaustion or a lack of joy in our lives.

Whole, well, happy people make effective peacemakers.

Cultivate Happiness

Being happy might not mean what you think it does. A growing body of research shows that happiness isn't an escape from pain, suffering, or adversity but rather a state of emotional wellbeing. Happiness is improved by navigating life's challenges, not avoiding them, and by building capacity for resilience and empathy, something that women who have had abortions and other stigmatized groups know a lot about. Additionally, living with a purpose greater than oneself improves people's individual lives and the lives of others.

Some themes that are emerging in the research on happiness include the following:

Happiness can be defined. It's a complex emotional phenomenon that is a state of emotional wellbeing. A sense of security, a good outlook, autonomy or control over our lives, good relationships, and skilled and meaningful activity can all make people feel happy.[2] Most important, feeling happy really matters to people, positively impacting their health and wellbeing in many ways.[3]

Avoiding pain in the pursuit of happiness doesn't work. Overcoming challenges and experiencing serious trauma may dampen happiness in the short term, but it can create a sense of meaning in life that is beneficial.[4] Living defensively by trying to evade hardship is stressful, aggravating, and annoying in the long-term.[5]

A "meaning mind-set" improves happiness. People who seek connections, give to others, are involved in pursuing a larger purpose, and can enjoy the "day-to-day, moment-to-moment" nature of meaning instead of expecting it to be a constant, universal state are more likely to experience happiness.[6]

Self-awareness is really important. Knowing oneself and being able to respond consciously helps people connect who they are with what they do.[7] Learning to practice empathy and forgiveness, and building resilience, helps people to feel happy.

History has already taught us many of the lessons now being documented through this new research on happiness. We know that it's possible to go through incredible hardship and come out joyful on the other side. Perhaps you have already done it in your own life or seen it done by others you know; and perhaps, like me, you have been inspired by the life stories of many of our world's most influential peaceful leaders.

Archbishop Desmond Tutu, who fought apartheid, advocated forgiveness, and led South Africa through its gutwrenching process of truth and reconciliation, is known worldwide for his humor and joy. His Holiness the Dalai Lama, living in exile from Tibet since 1959 and unable to visit his homeland, literally wrote the book on the art of happiness.[8] Gloria Steinem, despite being saddled with every media myth about the anger and aggression of feminists, is renowned for her wit and approachability.

Free of cynicism, these leaders appear as fresh and ready to address what's next as they did decades ago. Steinem celebrated her 80th birthday in 2014 with an article on why the feminist revolution was just getting started. She playfully explained to those who expect her to "pass the torch" of leadership that she plans to keep her torch, "thank you very much—and I'm using it to light the torches of others."[9]

In her simple analogy, Steinem illustrated the concept of abundance. There doesn't have to be one feminist leader at a time—there can be dozens, hundreds, if not thousands. No one needs to step down in order for someone else to step up; no one needs to diminish her own power or impact in order for others to have more. Of course, not everyone can be the next Gloria Steinem. Nor should they be. Cookie-cutter, one-size-fits-all molds aren't the goal. Breaking up the stereotypes and letting go of the labels that keep people from expressing their full selves is the aim.

Each person is unique and different. This is wonderful.

No fight or conflict, no matter how important its resolution is to you or your community, should define or limit your ability to honestly express yourself and experience happiness and joy. It is possible to heal—not forget, nor ignore—from your own personal pain, and you get to feel whole and well despite society's daily tragedies and horrors. Healing and wholeness are important to pro-voice practice because we value and prioritize the wellbeing of our community members and so that we don't use our own personal traumas as a reason or excuse to inflict more hurt and pain on the world.

Dealing with Pain

America's abortion wars have persisted for the same basic reason that most conflicts endure: people keep fighting. War is rarely about logic, reason, or policy. Conflicts are fueled by history, passion, pain, fear, and the social expectation that aggression should be met with a fierce response. It's natural for humans to push back when feeling persecuted or victimized, both to end current harm and to prevent future damage. And it works. Even when the original perpetrator can't be touched, humans can send a message that they "may be down but aren't out."[10] Those who retaliate get attacked less in the future.

As long as one side of the abortion wars keeps pushing, the other side is almost evolutionarily bound to keep fighting back, to keep showing the world that it isn't weak and won't quit, not ever. The pain and violence of these wars isn't just metaphorical, either; it's a lived experience. This is why laws and policy won't fix the conflict. Neither will just playing nice or encouraging civility, though they can help.

The tradition of pain passing—of an individual or group causing other individuals or groups pain in response to their own experience of pain—is present in all manner of human conflict, from family feuds and gang wars to international and interpersonal clashes. Everyone knows the parable of the man who comes home after a hard day at work, fuming from being yelled at by his boss, and who then yells at his wife, who yells at the kid, who kicks the dog. People who feel hurt often hurt others. People with racial and ethnic prejudices who feel pressured by declining economic and social resources often place blame for their troubles on individuals from marginalized groups. Immigrant bashing increases when a native population feels stretched thin. For example, in the case of Christian evangelist Jerry Falwell, his anger and hurt over the 9/11 attacks on America was quickly transferred into blaming the assault on the groups he hated most: "pagans, abortionists, feminists, lesbians."

Pain passing has gotten more creative, thanks to the Internet. Public shaming and relational aggression are two age-old strategies, facilitated anew by the speed and reach of social media. A double-edged sword, social media has the capacity to both expose wrongdoing and perpetuate it. Any way you slice it, it's a powerful tool.

Commenting in *Wired* magazine on the dangers of online public shaming, Laura Hudson called social media "a weapon of mass reputation destruction capable of amplifying slander, bullying, and casual idiocy on a scale never before possible."

She questioned the point at which shaming bullies online becomes bullying itself, with victims enduring real costs and real pain. She cautioned that Internet shaming campaigns are often "too brutal for the crime" and impossible to shut down.[11]

Online public shaming isn't the only modern weapon of cultural warfare made stronger by social media. Relational aggression—a covert, bullying act—works by damaging the important relationships of its targets, and it's easily manipulated with social networks. Instead of the direct confrontational attacks associated with public shaming, relational aggression relies on what goes unsaid, the behaviors that happen behind people's backs, such as gossip and social exclusion. In today's parlance, relational aggression is found in the "subtweet" and "side eye," actions designed to erode the credibility of their target.

Outspoken feminists have found themselves in their own cycle of pain passing. While online feminism was once considered an empowering and exciting development for the future, Michelle Goldberg revealed in her January 2014 cover story, "Feminism's Toxic Twitter Wars," for the Nation that it has turned "dysfunctional, even unhealthy." However one views the source of the conflicts, many of online feminism's leaders and members now call their public discussions "toxic." Former editor of the trendsetting blog Feministing Samhita Mukhopadhyay told Goldberg that the nastiness online has made everyone "scared to speak right now."

Katherine Cross, who is working on a PhD at the CUNY Graduate Center, described how relational aggression impacts feminist activists: it feels, she said, like "you're getting turned out of your own home." The safety and comfort of home is exactly what relational aggression aims to destroy. Respected feminists may feel "tarred by the very people" that they care about and have longstanding relationships with. Their most important relationships may be destroyed. "It's extremely damaging," said Cross.[12]

Brittney Cooper, an assistant professor at Rutgers and cofounder of the *Crunk Feminist Collective* blog, understands that the hostility that goes on between feminists is rooted in something real. "There's an actual injury," Cooper affirms.[13]

There always is.

"Historical experiences matter," wrote David P. Barash, PhD, and Judith Eve Lipton, MD, in *Payback: Why We Retaliate, Redirect Aggression, and Take Revenge*, "because such experiences, especially when painful, generate passions and animosities as well as a felt need for revenge and restitution in the present."[14] Dealing with the desire to seek revenge created by a history of painful experiences is one of the great challenges of every human society. "The world's great ethical systems have long struggled to define responses to victimization that preserve personal and collective security," wrote Barash and Lipton, "without falling into the excessive violence of unbridled payback."

Lipton and Barash poignantly asked in *Payback*, "How can a well-meaning person stop short of being a violent, pain-inflicting son of a bitch and yet also avoid being a sucker?"

How, indeed.

The cycle of pain passing can be transformed. But it demands that each person, and his or her group, take responsibility to absorb pain rather than cause more of it. We know the names of famous people, such as Nelson Mandela, Dr.

Martin Luther King Jr., and Mahatma Gandhi, who chose the path of love and respect over hate and retribution, but everyone is capable of choosing compassion for those who have caused great pain.

Sujatha Baliga, the incest survivor who laughed at His Holiness the Dalai Lama when he suggested that she align herself with her enemy, became a leading restorative-justice practitioner. Lucia McBath, the mother of 17-year old Jordan Davis, who was shot and killed sitting in a car listening to music with his friends, forgave her son's killer. "Don't think that I am not angry," she told Ta-Nehisi Coates of the *Atlantic*. "Forgiving Michael Dunn [Davis's killer] doesn't negate what I'm feeling. . . . But more than that I have a responsibility to God to walk the path He's laid . . . I am still called by the God I serve to walk this out."[15]

In 2010, after being forced to resign from the administration of President Barack Obama after fierce right-wing attacks led by conservative Fox commentator Glenn Beck, Van Jones accepted an award from the NAACP in Los Angeles. In his speech, Jones spoke directly to Beck: "I see you, and I love you, brother . . . I love you and you cannot do anything about it. Let's be one country. Let's get the job done." Four years later, Beck admitted on Fox News that he "made an awful lot of mistakes . . . I think I played a role, unfortunately, in helping tear the country apart." He went on about his regrets during the time he spent on the air between 2009 and 2011: "I wish I could go back and be more uniting in my language," Beck said. "I look back and I realize if we could have talked about the uniting principles a little bit more, instead of just the problems, I think I would look back on it a little more fondly."[16]

No one would describe people like Baliga, McBath, or Jones as passive or weak. They exude a strength and power that isn't based in aggression, violence, or fear. Their power is rooted in their vulnerability. It's evidenced by their courage to be open and loving despite their heartache. They show us a glimpse of humanity's better nature.

The example they set "does not mean meek submission to the will of the evil doer," as Gandhi has described nonviolent leadership; "it means pitting of one's whole soul against the will of the tyrant."[17]

Most great religions include ideas, strategies, and tools for forgiveness and reconciliation. Buddhism, in particular, is grounded in the recognition of human pain and suffering and the need to cultivate compassion. Christianity is steeped in forgiveness, and the message to love your enemy is carried throughout the Bible. In Islam, the Qur'an warns against victims' using their pain to become offenders and suggests that Allah rewards those who can make peace with those who have caused injury. An example of Jewish morality is found in the celebration of Passover, which includes a ritual that expresses regret that the liberation of the Jews required suffering on the part of their Egyptian oppressors. Orthodox Jews say a compassionate prayer before bed that asks God not to punish the people who have hurt them. Economists, psychiatrists, game theorists, and addiction specialists, such as Alcoholics Anonymous, have all developed theories and methods to use apology, meditation, breathing, and other coping strategies to escape pain passing and promote peace.[18]

An enduring fight like the abortion wars, waged over meaning, purpose, and group identity, requires a special kind of willingness to build bridges across deep and hostile divides. It demands awareness of the history of pain and struggle that has defined the lives of so many and a commitment not to pass that pain along. Caring about those who are different is perhaps the greatest fundamental challenge of humanity, especially when it requires offering compassion to one's enemy, respecting those on the other side of the political aisle, and choosing to accept suffering as an act of love.

Conscious suffering, the choice to absorb pain rather than pass it on through revenge or bullying, should not be confused with sacrifice. Suffering is an acknowledgment of reality. Given that pain can't be escaped, our responsibility is to not make it worse. We should use our words, our time, and our efforts to bring its counterbalance compassion and love—into the world to ease the burdens on our fellow humans. Sacrifice, on the other hand, is a choice to do without, to forgo something that is important, meaningful, and often emotionally or physically sustaining. It can be described as self-denial or abstinence.

If acceptance of suffering is a conscious decision to not cause more pain and an attempt to increase compassion in the world, then personal sacrifice is a conscious decision to deny yourself something you need on behalf of the greater good. Beware the damaging impact of sacrifice. Never, warned James Bevel, the respected civil rights leader, should one plunge into personal sacrifice alone, without a movement strategy.[19]

The emotional and psychological trauma that results from sustained sacrifice can do far more harm than good. Bitterness, resentment, and despair can result. It can lower morale, increase anger, lead to burnout, and facilitate victimhood. When one is exhausted, it becomes impossible to lead, think, or act with purpose. All that's left is basic survival. In that state, it is impossible to do the loving work of absorbing pain and offering compassion to an enemy.

You cannot pit your soul against the will of the tyrant if it is weakened by despair.

Cynicism is one of the great warning signs of burnout. When formerly passionate activists turn gloomy skeptics, they rarely seek healing, but they can attract new believers, often under the guise of pragmatism and reality, splintering the movement and taking others with them. Many environmentalists have accepted their own despair about the future of the planet. At just 41 years old, globally respected environmental activist Paul Kingsnorth has already left hope behind. He admitted, "Whenever I hear the word 'hope' these days, I reach for my whiskey bottle. . . . Surely we only hope when we are powerless?" Accepting defeat on climate change, Kingsnorth has moved his family to a remote area to distance themselves from civilization and begin to prepare for the worst that's to come.[20]

"We must actively guard against cynicism," asserted Raven Brooks, the executive director of Netroots Nation, which connects progressive grassroots activists. Because once activists get to this point, Brooks said, they have already lost their ability to "throw a Hail Mary or think about what's needed to change the game."[21]

Near the end of his life, Dr. King's hardest task was to prevent the swell of bitterness he saw increasing around him. He knew such despair led to self-pity that would "poison the soul and scar the personality." Dealing with disappointment was an "agonizing human experience," but still, he advised, one must cling to infinite hope.[22]

Eveline Shen, executive director of Forward Together, agrees that resisting self-pity is challenging. When she is under attack, she perceives her opponents—whether friends or enemies—in such a way that she can see their humanity. "Most of the time, when I'm having major conflict with people," Shen shares, "I always hold the possibility that things will change and maybe I will be working with them as allies in the future."[23]

It is not always easy to know when one is making an unnecessary sacrifice, the kind that leads to self-pity. "When I look back on my career," one reproductive rights activist told me, "I see that the times I told myself I was making a purposeful professional sacrifice were really the times I was making a leadership mistake. I was feeling pressure to make a certain kind of choice and I buckled. I wouldn't make those mistakes again." She isn't alone. It's common to justify a whole range of personal sacrifices under the cloak of professional choice, in the name of the greater good.

Instead of being tools to ease the burden of human suffering, these individual acts can actually create more pain by producing resentment and burnout. When the extent of an individual's sacrifice is concealed, when her burdens are not spoken about or collectively shared, these seemingly innocuous decisions can add up to an emotional death by a thousand cuts. Once resentment sets in, it's difficult for people to see or accept their own power to make change, especially when it comes to their own individual choices. They blame others for the sacrifices they chose to make. They become victims. If they don't stop their own sacrificial practice, it's likely that they will pass the pain along.

"Ultimately," said Raven Brooks, feelings of resentment from unacknowledged sacrifice "will ruin relationships and make you less effective as a person and change agent."[24] Hidden sacrifice "is the detriment of our movement," declared Eveline Shen. "It's exactly the opposite direction of what we need to change. It's not a powerful way to be."[25]

A Discipline of Self-Care

Social-justice movements, such as those for women's rights and racial equality, are legendary for the sacrifices of their leaders and members. Many have worked endless hours, met countless times, traveled nonstop, and led ongoing campaigns for "the work," neglecting their families, their health, and often their own need to feel happiness and joy.

Before he was assassinated, Dr. King worked 20-hour days, traveled approximately 325,000 miles annually, and often gave as many as 450 speeches per year.[26] It is an example that can't be matched and probably shouldn't be attempted. Yet this type of "tireless" effort has set a standard of expectation for many leaders and those who want to be a part of social change. Those who have experienced big losses and made big personal sacrifices often judge someone's value or commitment to the cause by how much he or she has sacrificed.

"It becomes about who sacrifices more for the cause," explained Shen. When sacrifice is the bond that binds community together, when it serves as the litmus test to entrance and acceptance in the group, and when it defines a way of life, sacrifice for the greater good becomes the end, rather than the means, for change.[27]

"A terrible waste" is how Akaya Windwood, executive director of the Rockwood Leadership Institute for nonprofit social-change leaders, described personal sacrifice.[28]

The pro-voice movement doesn't want to waste our leaders, our most precious resources; neither does it seek to rescue them from the chance to overcome their own challenges and build the resilience needed for wellbeing. The third way, the meaningful leadership path between sacrifice and futility, is part of the discipline of being pro-voice.

Activist and philanthropist Shira Saperstein spent years funding small, grassroots organizations working for social justice. She sees how the people who work in small organizations are asked to be everywhere all the time and face challenges in saying no. But over her 25-year career, she has seen that it is the organizations that are able to "build up a real deep expertise in a few issues and say no to doing everything on the rest" are the ones that succeed. When people take on too much, when they don't set clear and fewer priorities, Saperstein said, it is to "the detriment of the organization."[29]

Kirsten Moore, the former president and CEO of the Reproductive Health Technologies Project, learned a lot from her own past mistakes in making sacrifices. Now, she understands that "in order to lead, you have to make choices, set priorities, and invest resources. It requires focus and discipline."[30] Windwood agrees. She isn't willing to sacrifice herself for her job—which for her would mean working more than 60 hours a week, not seeing her partner, jeopardizing her friendships, disengaging with family, and never going on vacation—but she is "willing to do the work that's in front of me with discipline."[31]

It's critical to distinguish between the hard work that's needed to generate hope and possibility for social change and the work that is a personal sacrifice, which will trigger resentment and despair. It isn't the same for everyone. One person's hard work can be another person's sacrifice.

Sacred is the root word of *sacrifice*, Windwood reminds leaders. Knowing what is sacred to you and can't be given away is paramount to each person's ability to make the disciplined choices he or she needs to thrive.

Like many new young leaders, I learned these lessons the hard way. In the first years after our founding, Exhale wasn't operating in a focused, disciplined way to achieve our goals. The counseling strategy of "self-care"—a term we used to help a caller think through ways in which she could take care of herself, physically and emotionally, after an abortion—had been adopted by staff members, volunteers, and board members as a way to escape responsibility. If someone was tired or overwhelmed, she could claim the need for "self-care" and make it everyone else's job to fill the gap she left behind. There was no accountability to the team.

This cultural practice of "self-care" hurt morale, it hurt Exhale, and it hurt our ability to achieve our mission by creating resentment and, eventually, the burnout of everyone who didn't practice "self-care"—i.e., the people who took responsibility to get the job done. It didn't work that well for those who practiced "self-care" either, as they were just as likely to get burdened at the worst possible time by someone else's need to recover. We had put ourselves into a nasty cycle of burnout and recovery, and, worst of all, we set up a situation in which we could take care either of ourselves as individuals or of Exhale, but not both. We had pitted our personal needs against those of the organization. It's no wonder neither was thriving.

Exhale didn't make up this "self-care" tradition. It was what people were used to in the nonprofit world, and they brought their experiences to bear on Exhale. However, Exhale needed a better way to be an organization, a way that could meet the needs of both individuals and the organization. As a team, we took responsibility to redefine the meaning of "self-care." From then on, the term signified the ways in which people cared for themselves *and* for Exhale. The change was a choice to honor the importance of our work and to sharpen the focus required to make a lasting social impact.

Now, when I think of self-care, I don't think of just manicures and massages or vacations and walks in the park. Self-care is not a simple feel-good activity. It's a much deeper and, ultimately, more meaningful tool: self-care is a discipline that honors what is sacred, including the hard work that provides meaning in our lives.

Since Exhale's own internal cultural transformation away from sacrifice and toward purpose nearly a decade ago, our organization has continued to learn lessons, adapt, and innovate our leadership practices. Here are a few examples of how Exhale has become more disciplined at pursuing our mission while honoring what's sacred to the people we work with:

> *We honor our talkline callers by respecting their unique challenges.* It can be incredibly difficult to listen to someone else going through a hard time. It's natural to want to save someone from her pain or hurt and wish she didn't have to go through it. Yet, rarely does

emotional rescue help out the other person. It may make it worse, and it can hurt the person doing the rescuing too. We believe in the strengths of our callers to overcome whatever adversity they are facing, and we are willing and able to listen, to serve as their witness, to be a sounding board and a thought partner. But we draw the line at carrying their burden for them. If we did, we'd miss out on being able to hear the joy and healing they find on the other side.

One woman, Joann, shared this about her call to the talkline: "After 45 years of not talking at all to anyone, I used Exhale's phone counseling and spoke about my abortions. I am now able to tell my story out loud, one carefully chosen person at a time. Each time I tell my story, it is with fewer tears. Thanks for giving me the courage and encouragement to use my voice to start to heal."

We respect the leadership and commitment of our volunteers. Few things are worse than feeling that someone has wasted your time or not taken you seriously, especially when you have carved time out of your life to give to others. Over the years, Exhale has made the volunteer talkline commitment more rigorous and more demanding, but rather than losing volunteers, we have more applying to our program than we can accept. Volunteers want to be a part of Exhale because we've built a reputation for being serious and respectful of their commitment and because we offer them something that's tough to find: a meaningful opportunity to make a difference in the world.

One volunteer commented about her experience with Exhale: "I'm a natural leader. . . . What's so great about Exhale is it allowed me to recognize that, made me feel like a legit leader because that's how they treat me. They put together these professional retreats, honor my opinions and ideas in a way that [is] empowering."

We build community so that leaders can take big risks. Sharing emotionally vulnerable stories with strangers, staying open and creative when feeling under attack, providing compassion to the enemy, and accepting suffering as an act of love are all incredibly difficult challenges, and yet each one is crucial to the mission of transforming the abortion conflict. These acts shouldn't be attempted alone. Pro-voice community gives leaders the confidence and support needed to step outside their comfort zones and live in the gray areas.

Describing a pre-tour leadership retreat, one fellow remarked, "That feeling in the room all weekend of complete support and compassion and love, [it] made me feel whatever happened on tour, knowing these people were going to be there, I could do it."

We ask a great deal of the staff, leadership, and board of Exhale, but we never ask that the people who work here give up their own happiness, sacrifice what is sacred to them, or bear the burdens of others because we know that victims, rescuers, and sacrificers hurt themselves and jeopardize mission impact. We require ourselves to offer love and compassion to those outside Exhale, to those inside, and to ourselves. Pro-voice, after all, is a life philosophy, not just something we do at work.

Making sure that Exhale's culture and expectations are a match for people who want to work with us is also one of the ways we honor where people are coming from and what they need in their own lives. For example, when we interview people for volunteer or paid positions, we always ask them about what is called a "peak experience." We want to know how they felt during a specific time when all their systems were at go, when they were firing on all cylinders, when they came alive and felt like they were at their best, living their best life, and at home in their own skin. When someone describes being at her best making sense of chaos, surmounting something she never thought possible, connecting previously disparate ideas or people, or finding a way to communicate through noise, it's clear how to connect her with the role that best meets Exhale's needs and makes her come alive with purpose. This is how we cultivate purpose and happiness at Exhale.

We don't find joy by avoiding pain and trauma, by retreating from the challenges and obstacles we face, or by making others feel our hurts. We find it by knowing ourselves very well and putting our unique talents and strengths to use in ways that further the mission of Exhale and the personal and professional growth of the people we work with.

Make Pro-Voice Your Own

A life of purpose, surrounded by a community of kindred spirits who honor what's sacred and cultivate happiness through resilience and empathy, is the promise of the pro-voice movement for those who want to make it their daily practice.

However you come to pro-voice—whether as a person with an abortion experience, as someone with your own hidden story, or as an ally—you are encouraged to make it your own, expanding the reach and influence of its core values. Some readers may be ready to adopt pro-voice as a way of life immediately, while others may just want to experiment with some of its tools.

Pro-voice tools are applicable in every instance of human interaction, from talking with a friend or family member and dealing with coworkers or neighbors to engaging with advocates who work on the opposite side of your issue. Whether you are taking the leap to tell someone about your abortion for the first time or you are ready to take the risk to explore the gray areas of a controversial subject, the following strategies and tools can help you move forward with respect, resilience, and empathy for yourself and others.

Pro-voice people come from all walks of life and from a wide variety of political views, and yet they all have a few things in common. Pro-voice people live their lives with purpose. They need to help make the world a better place.

They also connect with kindred spirits, finding and creating communities of people who share their passions. And pro-voice people are extremely self-aware because they want to grow and improve themselves as human beings. Beyond these shared characteristics, pro-voice people use the following tools:

For more free pro-voice tools, please visit:
www.exhaleprovoice.org

Listening

The simple act of genuinely listening to another person is powerful and is at the heart of pro-voice practice. Listen with your full attention. Listen without judgment or assumptions. Simply listen. If you are listening to someone share about a difficult or traumatic experience, remember that each individual already has her own internal and environmental strengths to support her wellbeing. Be a sounding board and brainstorm options instead of giving advice or telling the person what to feel or do. Being a great listener doesn't mean you're an emotional doormat either, so negotiate boundaries to keep you and the other person emotionally healthy and strong. Setting appropriate limits is an integral part of caring and effective communication.[32]

> *Use open-ended questions.* Invite someone to share in detail about what she's going through by asking questions that let her explore and reveal her truths, in her own ways, rather than using closed-ended questions

that can be answered only by yes or no. Ask "What are you feeling?" instead of "Do you feel all right?" Open-ended questions can also help connect people to their own inner strength. When a listener asks questions like "What has worked in the past?" "How do you like to take care of yourself?" and "What do you feel good doing?" he can help a person to uncover past and present successes that may help her to address her current challenges.

Use reflective language. Using phrases such as "I hear you're feeling . . ." or "It sounds to me like . . ." coupled with more tentative statements like "I wonder if you're feeling . . . ?" or "Did I get that right?" helps people to name what they are experiencing, invites them to correct your understanding, and conveys your sincere interest in what they have to say. When you reflect back the language that people use to describe their own experience, you meet them on their own ground. Some abortion-related words to keep in mind as you listen to someone's specific language include "baby," "procedure," "spirit," and "unborn child." Similarly, remember that certain faith-related terms mean different things to different people. For example, "God" and "the Lord" may represent two very different concepts. Using the same words as the speaker lets her know that you respect her point of view, even if it's not your own.

Validate personal experience. When listening to individuals from stigmatized or marginalized experiences, it is critical that you validate their personal experience. Remember that the impact of stigma causes people to feel like they are alone or like they are the only ones, and they worry that others may think they are crazy or not normal. When you listen to their stories, it is not the time to engage in a political fight or an academic argument. Your primary role is to help an individual to feel heard, without judgment. Whether it is a woman who has had an abortion sharing her emotions or a person of color describing his experiences of racism, let them know that you believe them.

Storytelling

There is an art and a craft to storytelling that can be intimidating for people who find it hard to believe they have any story worth sharing, especially if it's about something personal, taboo, or hidden. Pro-voice storytelling isn't about the most persuasive, perfect narrative; it's focused on the act of one person telling her own story, in her own words, in her own time, rather than having others speak on her behalf. When done ethically, storytelling practices support an individual's ability to think through what it is she wants to say, whom she wants to say it to, and what she hopes will happen as a result, while retaining significant control over the use and distribution of her narrative. Whether she wants her story to stay private or reach the biggest possible audience, what's most important is that the storyteller feels—and is— heard. Storytelling venues and distribution look very different when this goal is central to storytelling practices. Feeling heard, supported, and respected is key to ending the isolating impact of stigma while building the confidence needed for new pro-voice challenges—such as accepting that what makes a story powerful is that listeners may come to a different conclusion.[33]

> *Practice ethical storytelling.* A woman who is an equal partner with an advocate, who is able to direct when and how her story will be used, and who has full decision-making power over the advocacy agenda in which her story is used is a woman in an empowered position. On the other hand, it is a form of exploitation to take all or part of a story from a woman and use it for advocacy purposes without receiving her consent or without empowering her with the authority to make decisions about how her story is used. Therefore, advocates working on behalf of the health, safety, rights, and justice of women and their families are obliged to create story-sharing processes and decision-making structures that empower community members with real authority.

> *Know the risks and benefits.* After sharing a story, a storyteller might feel empowered and more connected to others, such as her family or others who have had abortions. Sharing stories can strengthen bonds with family and friends; it can help a person not feel so alone; and it can generate more social support for other people with a shared experience. Sharing can also come with great personal and professional risks. After telling an intimate story, a person may feel vulnerable or more alone than she did before. Others may try to shame or hurt her, or try to use her story against

her. Rather than strengthening family ties, sharing can threaten the stability of relationships and jobs. Be aware that political and religious organizations may be interested in a personal story as a way to influence people toward their position. However a storyteller aligns politically, remember that her story is hers to keep. No one should ever feel pressured, coerced, or shamed into telling her story, even if it's to promote a cause she believes in.

Use whole stories, not talking points. Stories, as all advocates know, are powerful tools. Stories have the ability to persuade, influence, inspire, and galvanize people to action. This power is so strong and so coveted that many advocates talk about collecting and distributing stories as if they were commodities to be bought and sold. Advocates' increased focus on capturing a story and having it told in public can often leave out a crucial element of story sharing: the storyteller. Human, vulnerable, authentic personal stories don't fit easily into talking points, but they have incredible power to connect with others across differences. Advocates have an important role to play in creating the conditions necessary for a storyteller to feel encouraged and supported to share her whole truth, and once those conditions exist, advocates can benefit from compelling story sharing.

Embrace Gray Areas

Gray areas are one of the greatest sources for innovation and creative thinking, and exploring them is a tactic that Exhale has used time and time again. Whether it was filling the need for nonpartisan postabortion support, developing e-cards to spur intimate conversations between loved ones, or promoting the wellbeing of abortion storytellers, Exhale's most trendsetting programs were established by acknowledging and exploring the tensions between black and white. Our ability to ask the right questions and pursue learning and insight, rather than answers, is what has opened the door for new ways of thinking about stuck issues. For example, given the success of the Sharing Our Stories Tour and the knowledge that what made the pro-voice events successful was their small size, we already know that expanding our success won't mean having bigger, more public events. So, we ask instead, "How do we scale intimacy to preserve the intimate nature that helps people connect while creating more opportunities for people to participate?"

> *Practice a both/and approach (instead of either/or).* After a woman has an abortion, she can feel both relief and sadness, as well as many other combinations of emotions that may at first glance seem inconsistent. She may want to keep it private and need emotional connections with other women. A person can own a gun and want to prevent gun violence, and a political opponent can be both respected and challenged for his beliefs. When we hold space for multiple experiences and truths to live together simultaneously, we are living honestly in the gray areas.

Change your perspective. Sure, it may be easier if the
whole world saw the issue in the same way you do, but
that's not realistic or very interesting. Conflict exists
because we are human, and because our different backgrounds, values, and beliefs mean that we perceive the
world and its issues in unique, diverse ways. Hold space
for universal human truths—such as our shared ability
to be compassionate and loving—and recognize some
experiences as specific and particular, such as the experience of women with street harassment or of black men
with the police, which may be different from your own.
For over a decade, Eveline Shen has grown Forward
Together from its beginnings as an Oakland-based
Asian-American-centered organization to a national,
multiracial movement-building one innovating strategies to improve the health and rights of communities
of color. She credits her ability to sit in the gray areas
with her ability to broaden Forward Together's mission
and reach, because it gives her "much more of a chance
to see things differently." Gray areas, says Shen, can help
you "relate to people who are not exactly like you."[34]

Practice Self-Care

No movement worth its salt should demand that its members sacrifice themselves for the cause (without this sacrifice being a stated, movement-wide strategy, shared by all);
nor should burnout, exhaustion, or overwhelm be the price
to pay for working to make the culture more fair, equal,
and just. To build the world we want, we must practice

the behaviors that embody our values and our aspirations today, even against great odds. A culture capable of loving and respecting each other across our differences requires a strict discipline of self-care.[35]

> *Know what's sacred.* Know yourself well enough to know what causes you to be resentful and burned out, and honor your own wellbeing by refusing to sacrifice it away. This is easier said than done, and like most things, it's a practice that can be improved over time. First, notice when you feel resentful or overwhelmed. Instead of blaming someone else for how you feel and becoming a victim of the situation, reflect on the moment you felt like you gave something away, the time you buckled, or the time you went against your gut for what you felt was the right thing to do. Is this a common challenge you find yourself in? Have you been there before? What would it take to make a different choice next time? Your wellbeing is incredibly valuable, so what can you do to treat yourself with the honor you deserve?
>
> *Cultivate happiness.* You get to be happy, well, and whole no matter how broken the world is. You deserve happiness. The pro-voice movement cares about your wellbeing because happiness is integral to the more supportive, respectful culture we are building. As a community, we champion one another's happiness by believing in each other's ability to build resilience and overcome adversity without rescuing each other from pain or passing it along to hurt others.

Not everyone will have an abortion. Not everyone will experience rape or domestic abuse. Not everyone is gay or an immigrant. Not everyone is stricken by mental illness or disability. And, certainly, not everyone is of the same skin color, race, or ethnicity, even if we pretend the differences don't matter. Pro-voice tools are designed to help people actively care about people who are different from ourselves or who have experiences that don't seem to touch or impact our own daily lives. They are an act of resistance against apathy, defensiveness, and empty outrage. When practiced, pro-voice tools help us to care.

Caring about others is more important than ever. In *The New Jim Crow: Mass Incarceration in the Age of Colorblindness*, Michelle Alexander pointed out,

> When people think about crime, especially drug crime, they do not think about suburban housewives violating laws regulating prescription drugs or white frat boys using ecstasy. Drug crime in this country is understood to be black and brown, and it is because drug crime is racially defined in the public consciousness that the electorate has not cared much what happens to drug criminals—at least not the way they would have cared if the criminals were understood to be white. It is this failure to care, really care across color lines, that lies at the core of this system of control and every racial caste system that has existed in the United States or anywhere else in the world.[36]

What's Next for Exhale and Pro-Voice

During Exhale's 2013 Sharing Our Stories Tour, our Pro-Voice fellows met people of all ages and from a wide array of racial, ethnic, and religious backgrounds and political beliefs. They talked with pro-choice and pro-life audiences, and they listened as people openly shared their own personal, hidden stories. While most people they spoke to did not have an abortion experience to discuss, they did have some kind of story that connected them to the fellows. Whether it was living with a rare disease, dealing with the death of a loved one, or attempting to bridge conflicts within their own families and communities, audience members knew the desire to open up and be treated with respect. We all do.

Exhale heard the need loud and clear: there is a demand to adopt and apply pro-voice tools beyond the issue of abortion. We aim to deliver.

Exhale is pursuing our vision of a world with less separation and more ability to reach across difference to bring peace. Abortion will remain Exhale's core issue while we build a network of pro-voice champions who can connect and amplify the power of pro-voice in new arenas. We seed the pro-voice movement beyond abortion by making pro-voice tools freely available. We invest in peacemakers and provide a platform for all pro-voice experts the people whose lived experiences are often hidden behind the fight.

The opportunities for expanding pro-voice abound.

When it comes to abortion, there are two related areas of personal experience where adopting a pro-voice perspective has the potential to dramatically shift the debate, instilling more empathy, compassion, and understanding: validating emotions and promoting wellbeing.

> *Abortion regret and relief.* While pro-life postabortion groups publicly acknowledge that a woman can heal and move on from the pain and regret of her abortions, pro-choice groups remain reticent to address it at all. Yet, I can't think of a more pro-choice issue than abortion regret. *Regret is inherent to personal choice and individual freedoms.* Preventing people from experiencing regret is easy: take away their choice. In this, the pro-life strategy of wanting to outlaw abortion because women might regret having one is completely consistent with their values and goals. On the other hand, the pro-choice movement has yet to publicly accept that if they truly trust a woman to make these choices for themselves, then they must also accept that a woman can make the wrong one. Rather than minimizing regret, the pro-choice movement could show their unwavering commitment to the value of choice by acknowledging, accepting, and providing emotional support to those who wish they had never had an abortion. The pro-choice movement could turn their perceived biggest vulnerability into one of their most notable strengths. On the flip side, it is critical that the pro-life movement acknowledge that a woman can have a range of reactions to her abortion, and they can include positive, life-affirming, and confidence-building emotions, such as relief, gratitude, and renewed hope for the future. One can still be opposed to abortion without pathologizing the women who have them

as mentally ill. Dr. C. Everett Koop, the surgeon general under President Ronald Reagan, who testified in 1989 that there was not enough scientific evidence to show that abortion emotionally harms women, is an important example of how a pro-life advocate can be against abortion and recognize that the procedure alone doesn't *cause* psychological damage.

Abortion stigma and wellbeing. A syndrome-free abortion and an abortion-stigma-free culture do not mean an emotionless abortion experience. The simple difference between a culture with stigma and pathology and one without is not whether people have feelings about their abortions but whether a woman feels able to express her emotions, safely. Listening without judgment and sharing hidden stories dismantle the barriers that keep people isolated from one another and open up new avenues for women to connect around their shared experiences. Given what's known about the role of our emotions in our ability to experience happiness—from the critical importance of self-awareness to the value of resilience in the face of adversity—*every woman who has an abortion should be getting assurance from all sides that whether her abortion was the best or worst choice of her life, it is possible for her to experience wellbeing afterward.* An abortion could be the emotional adversity a woman must find a way to overcome, or it could be the decision that saved her from a life of irreversible adversity; either way, she can build the resilience she needs through her ability to identify and cope with her emotions and rely on a network of support. The most important people in the work to shift the culture away from stigma and pathology and toward wellbeing are women who have had abortions; they should choose to treat other people's experiences with support and respect, especially if those experiences are different from their own. The woman who feels sorrow after her abortion is not the enemy of the one who feels calmed, nor is the one who chooses to keep her experience a secret the foe of the one who can't stop talking about hers. When women can see each other as allies across their abortion differences, listen to each other, and model empathy, they promote wellbeing for all.

Beyond abortion, advocates and allies have approached Exhale about their interest in using pro-voice in a number of arenas. These are the ones that I'm most excited about:

Gender and race. The emerging visibility of transgender people and the killings of unarmed black boys and young men such as Oscar Grant, Trayvon Martin, Jordan Davis, and Michael Brown mark critical cultural moments that demand a shift in our social norms, away from violence and fear of difference and toward safety and caring. To ensure the health and rights of America's most targeted and vulnerable citizens requires that we overcome the divides perpetuated by racism and heterosexism. Pro-voice tools can help people listen to those whose lived experience of their gender or race is different from their own.

Polarizing politics. Climate change and gun-violence prevention may sound like topics that need to be solved

by legislators and regulators, but behind each controversy are hidden personal stories—of science and faith,
nature and work, family and lifestyle, and pain and
trauma. Facts and figures can't resolve how to move
forward, but our ability to grasp the nuances and lay-
ers of the human stories behind the fight can.

Online communications. Social media can shift public
opinion in a single tweet. The new power and influence
that individual voices hold is incredible, and yet the
toxic, shaming, blaming mob mentality of social media
can destroy people, reputations, wellbeing, businesses,
and careers without due process. As the old saying goes,
"With great power comes great responsibility." If every
person now has a public voice, then the scope and tenor
of public debate is within our control to shape. Use pro-
voice tools online to affirm human dignity and invite
openness, engagement, and conversation.

Forgiveness and redemption. America loves a good apology, a rehabilitated villain. We embrace those who
admit and learn from their past misdeeds and move on
to help prevent others from making the same mistakes.
Former addicts and alcoholics support those trying to
kick their habits. Former gang members and murderers pay the price for their crimes and become shining
lights in their communities, helping wayward youth
choose better than they did. Former abusers of women,
children, and animals become teachers and advocates
for safety and respect. Can our culture support our cru-
elest transgressors—our racist killers and sexist rapists—
in moving beyond their worst deeds? Can we encourage

people like George Zimmerman, Michael Dunn, and Darren Wilson to transform themselves into antiracists who can use the example of their mistakes to help prevent the future killings of black boys, or will we keep them locked up as symbolic of our most hated enemies?

Atlantic senior editor and blogger Ta-Nehisi Coates took his 13-year-old son to hear Lucia McBath speak. McBath is the mother of Jordan Davis, a 17-year-old black boy who was killed by a white man while sitting in a car listening to music with friends in Florida. Coates took his son to hear McBath speak because his own son was "about the age when a black boy begins to directly understand what his country thinks of him. His parents cannot save him. His parents cannot save both his person and his humanity."

When McBath spoke to Coates's son later, she reminded him that above all else, above the racism, the fear, the hurt, and the uncertainty of his future, he continues to have every right to be himself, no matter what. "You exist," she told him. "You matter. You have value. You have every right to wear your hoodie, to play your music as loud as you want. You have every right to be you. And no one should deter you from being you. *You have to be you.* And you can never be afraid of being you."

After Darren Wilson, the white police offer who killed the unarmed black teenager Michael Brown in Ferguson, Missouri, was freed from any indictment of his behavior in November 2014, an emotional image went viral. At a protest against the Ferguson decision in Portland, Oregon, a young black boy carried a sign offering free hugs. When a white police officer took him up on his offer, the picture of the pair's embrace captured hearts, minds, and imaginations about what else is possible in the relationship between white cops and black boys. The boy, Devonte Hart, has a much bigger story to tell beyond that one picture. He was born addicted to drugs, was adopted by two moms, and by all accounts has become a beacon of light, defying odds left and right. When his mother shared details of Devonte's story with a local reporter, she described a scene at grocery store where two white adults asked him about his athletic prowess, assuming that because he was black, he played sports. At just 12 years old, Devonte responded that he had very different plans for his life than being an athlete. When he grows up, he told the two adults, "I'm going to be myself. No matter how much people try to make me something I am not."[37]

Being oneself can be the most vulnerable, courageous, peaceful, and important pro voice act in the world.

Conclusion

I was born at home, in a trailer, on the third anniversary of *Roe v. Wade*. The irony—or serendipity—that the day of my birth coincided with the Supreme Court decision that would have allowed my mother to legally end her pregnancy is not lost on me. Since starting Exhale, my birthday has never felt like my own.

A year into running Exhale, I was invited to sit on a panel at the Commonwealth Club in San Francisco to discuss the state of abortion politics in honor of *Roe v. Wade*. Because I was going to spend the evening talking about abortion, my then-boyfriend (now husband) met me for lunch to celebrate my birthday in downtown Oakland. We were having burgers across the plaza from City Hall when we noticed a small group of pro-life protestors who were picketing with their signs of a bloodied, dismembered fetus and saw the news vans there to catch the spectacle. Seeing them, I was gripped with fear and anxiety. I was scared and intimated, hurt and saddened. My boyfriend and I had to move and sit far away from the windows facing City Hall, where I tried unsuccessfully to enjoy myself.

I thought, "Why the hell did I decide to do this with my job? With my life? I must be f---ing crazy. Why in the world would I want to go out in public and talk about abortion?" As I was backed into a corner—literally sitting in the farthest corner of the restaurant—my natural fight-or-flee instinct kicked in, fiercely. I wanted to make the protestors feel like I did. I wanted to hurt and intimidate them. I wanted to yell at them, to tell them they were wrong and that I was a human person with feelings and that they were cruel, heartless animals. I also wanted to run for my life. My body wanted to take flight from my responsibilities that night at the Commonwealth Club, from Exhale, and from any future ideas I had to talk about my abortion in public. I wanted to leave it all behind.

This is how conflict works. It's effective at sweeping anyone it touches into its bitter, us-versus-them, war mentality. It demands an either/or decision. Wading into the waters of the debate without feeling the immense pressure to fight or to flee is practically impossible.

I was raw. Vulnerable. Emotional. I had no idea how, but I was more determined than ever to find a third way. I wanted to be able to be in the center of the conflict and be able to take a stand for peace and empathy despite the pressures of enemy thinking.

This is what I remember every year on my birthday, the anniversary of *Roe v. Wade*. The date is a reminder of a decision I made long ago to notice when the conflict sucks me into its dysfunction and of my choice to create another path. To this day, I feel those same pressures, that same human instinct to fight or flee, to hurt back and defend myself. Or to go make a quiet life for myself in some idyllic mountain town. There is no escape from these trains of thought, my human instinct. It is normal. To get through it, I remember my pro-voice values, I rely on my pro-voice community, and I practice my pro-voice tools.

I listen instead of fight.

The fight over abortion is not over. Harmful though it has been, I don't suggest that it should disappear altogether. What I want to change is the way that we are in conflict with each other. I believe it is culture—our social norms, our values and practices, the way we talk with one another, and our relationships—more than politics that is the most powerful opportunity we have to transform the public debate about abortion, making it more supportive of the people who have experienced abortions.

The tools of listening, storytelling, and embracing gray areas allow us to connect personally and intimately across our divides and to design a future debate that is rooted in mutual respect. Positive change is taking place. Conversations about abortion are already becoming more and more pro voice:

> *Listening* to the diverse experiences that people have with abortion has grown, thanks to the evolution of pro-life and pro-choice postabortion emotional-support services and the emergence of the full-spectrum doula movement.
>
> *Storytelling* about personal abortion experiences has exploded, thanks to online social sharing, individuals' increasing comfort with the public self-expression of their private tales, and more organizations and venues that welcome personal stories.
>
> *Embracing gray areas* helps media and entertainment outlets present abortion to their audiences with emotional honesty, and it helps political organizations such as Planned Parenthood and Forward Together to reach out beyond their base.

None of these exciting cultural changes would be happening without women who have had abortions taking the lead, shaping what's next. Driven by their shared experiences of abortion, women are now in the front seat, showing their faces to the public. It is their willingness to be seen that is the biggest challenge to abortion stigma and political conflict and the most inspiring development in the effort to generate social respect and peace.

Frustrated by the status quo, women are directly confronting the culture of stigma and shame that has kept their stories hidden and neglected behind the conflict for so many years. The most successful, influential work is being done out of love, compassion, and respect for other women, motivated by a desire to ensure that every woman who has an abortion—as well as her loved ones—feels heard, supported, and connected to a broader community of people who know what it's like to go through one. They're translating their anger and outrage at feeling isolated and alone into an emerging empathetic movement of women and men who are not just passionate about sharing their own stories—they are actively committed to listening to the stories of others.

One of the most dramatic changes in this regard is the new willingness of public leaders to talk openly about their abortions. Advocates for Youth, a national organization promoting sexual and reproductive health and rights for youth, hosted a revolutionary event in November 2014, a live-streamed abortion speak-out featuring prominent reproductive-justice leaders sharing their stories. Many, like Planned Parenthood's president, Cecile Richards, have been working on abortion rights for years but have only recently begun to open up about their own experiences. Richards joined

Advocates' own president, Debra Hauser; Jessica González-Rojas of the National Latina Institute for Reproductive Health; Yamani Hernandez of the Illinois Caucus for Adolescent Health; and others to connect the dots between their personal stories and their public leadership.

It is my hope that the storytelling of these reproductive-justice leaders not only changes the conversation about abortion but has an even broader impact on the role of women's personal stories in the public space. By talking openly about their private lives, they are charting a new course, realigning and renegotiating what makes the personal political. Thanks to their collective efforts, I imagine a future where a woman won't have to choose between showing herself as strong or vulnerable, courageous or afraid, professional or private. She must be only, proudly and compassionately, herself, faults and all.

Inspiring examples of women who have had abortions who are taking the lead in changing the culture around abortion to make it more empathetic include the following:

- Melissa Madera, *The Abortion Diary* podcast. A decade after her own abortion, Madera started the podcast in 2013 because she wanted to listen to other women's stories, to literally hear their voices. She travels the country so that she can be there in person when a woman shares her story, creating intimate connections through her listening that make sure each woman she talks to feels heard without judgment.

- Debra Hauser, president and CEO, Advocates for Youth. Under her leadership, Advocates initiated the "1 in 3 Campaign" in 2011 to support public abortion storytelling efforts designed to increase support for abortion care. Hauser launched the program with a video sharing her own story about abortion, and while the campaign's goals are political, they are committed to being a platform that honors and supports the full range of emotions and experiences.

* Maya Pindyck, Project Voice. Started in 2005 because Pindyck couldn't find personal narratives online, Project Voice is a platform for women to share their stories. Pindyck knows that the polarizing political language about abortion doesn't leave much room for personal stories, so her oral history project welcomes every kind of story a woman wants to tell.

There has never been a better time to have public conversations about personal abortion experiences.

Changes in media and technology have shifted expectations for how to participate in social-change efforts. Instead of just fighting to influence the whims of powerful institutions, people—especially the millennial generation—expect to be active participants in crafting the world around them. In fact, three out of four millennials believe that their generation is "starting a movement to change old, outdated systems." If something isn't working, such as the iconic American Dream or the decades-long abortion wars, millennials are less likely to complain and more prone to "take it upon themselves to create the next version of America."[1] Additionally, millennials value what pro-voice values: authenticity, creativity, connection, and most of all self-expression. The first generation to grow up with the Internet, millennials have few hang-ups about putting themselves out there for the world to see. "The biggest put-down in the millennial world," says one expert, "is to call someone fake."[2] What millennials have in common is "a level of optimism that most people think is silly."[3]

I certainly don't. A vibrant culture defined by authenticity, creativity, self-expression, and a can-do attitude to see the opportunities for innovation in the obstacles of enduring problems, such as the abortion conflict, is a pro-voice one.

Let's make it happen.

Notes

Preface

1. Guttmacher Institute, "Fact Sheet: Induced Abortion in the United States," July 2014, http://www.guttmacher.org/pubs/fb_induced_abortion.html.

2. During a televised forum in 2008, Christian pastor Rick Warren asked presidential candidates Barak Obama and John McCain when a baby gets "human rights"; http://blogs.reuters.com/talesfromthetrail/2008/08/16/obama-says-pointed-abortion-query-above-his-pay-grade/.

Chapter 1, The Birth of Pro-Voice

1. "History of Operation Rescue," http://en.wikipedia.org/wiki/History_of_Operation_Rescue.

2. My mother's second husband, Chris Evans, served as Surfrider's executive director from 1999 to 2004.

3. Martin Luther King Jr., *A Testament of Hope: The Essential Writings and Speeches of Martin Luther King, Jr.*, ed. James Melvin Washington (New York: HarperCollins Publishers, 1986), 628.

4. Frances Kissling, "Is there life after Roe? How to think about the fetus," *Conscience* 25, no 3 (Winter 2004–2005), https://www.catholicsforchoice.org/news/pr/2005/documents/c2004win_lifeafterroe.pdf.

5. Anna Quindlen, "Life Begins at Conversation," *Newsweek*, November 28, 2004, http://www.newsweek.com/life-begins-conversation 124709.

6. On May 17, 2009, Obama gave the commencement speech at Notre Dame, in which he tackled the subject of abortion amid protests; http://www.washingtonpost.com/wp-dyn/content/article/2009/05/17/AR2009051701622.html.

7. Exhale worked with Learning for Action to develop a theory of change and a logic model to measure the social impact of our program. An infographic with the results of the evaluation can be found on the Exhale website, https://exhaleprovoice.org/feature/how-stopthestigma.

8. David P. Barash and Judith Eve Lipton, *Payback: Why We Retaliate, Redirect Aggression, and Take Revenge* (New York: Oxford University Press, 2011), 77.

Chapter 2, America's Abortion Conflict

1. Jane E. Brody, "Abortion: Once a Whispered Problem, Now a Public Debate," *New York Times*, January 8, 1968, http://query.nytimes.com/mem/archive/pdf?res=9D02E0D6173BE73ABC4053DFB7668383679EDE.

2. Gene Roberts, "New Leaders and New Course for 'Snick,'" *New York Times*, May 21, 1966, http://query.nytimes.com/mem/archive/pdf?res=F20917F6345A117B93C0AB178ED85F428685F9.

3. Suzanne Staggenborg, *The Pro-Choice Movement: Organization and Activism in the Abortion Conflict* (New York: Oxford University Press, 1991), 45.

4. Brody, "Abortion: Once a Whispered Problem, Now a Public Debate."

5. Staggenborg, *The Pro-Choice Movement*, 28.

6. Ibid., 24.

7. Leslie Reagan, *When Abortion Was a Crime: Women, Medicine, and Law in the United States, 1867–1973* (Berkeley: University of California Press, 1997), 224.

8. This interview is a selection from "This is an Emergency Print Portfolio"—an art and writing portfolio project curated in 2012 by Meredith Stern. For more information about the project and to purchase the collection, go to Justseeds: Justseeds Collaborations: This is an Emergency! http://meredith-stern.tumblr.com/post/28101247220/i-was-born-in-1945-into-a-very-loving-and-caring.

9. Jael Silliman et al., *Undivided Rights: Women of Color Organize for Reproductive Justice* (Cambridge, MA: South End Press, 2004), 7.

10. Ibid., 54.

11. Ibid., 8.

12. Jael Silliman and Anannya Bhattacharjee, *Policing the National Body: Race, Gender, and Criminalization* (Cambridge, MA: South End Press, 2002), 125.

13. Angela Davis, *Women, Race & Class* (New York: Vintage Books, 1983), 204–206.

14. Linda B. Bourque, *A Biographical Essay on Judith Blake's Professional Career and Scholarship*, 1995, http://www.annualreviews.org/doi/pdf/10.1146/annurev.so.21.080195.002313.

15. Staggenborg, *The Pro-Choice Movement*, 38.

16. Lucinda Cisler, "Unfinished Business: Birth Control and Women's Liberation," in *Sisterhood Is Powerful: An Anthology of Writings from the Women's Liberation Movement* (New York: Vintage Books, 1970).

17. Staggenborg, *The Pro-Choice Movement*, 30.

18. Kristin Luker, *Abortion and the Politics of Motherhood* (Berkeley: University of California Press, 1984), 142.

19. Ibid.,127.

20. Ibid., 144.

21. Ibid.

22. Ibid., 126.

23. Ibid.

24. Ibid., 137.

25. Kissling, "Is There Life After Roe? How to Think About the Fetus."

26. Luker, *Abortion and the Politics of Motherhood*, 224.

27. Elizabeth Nash et al., *Laws Affecting Reproductive Health and Rights: 2013 State Policy Review*, Guttmacher Institute, 2013, https://www.guttmacher.org/statecenter/updates/2013/statetrends42013.html.

28. Ibid.

29. Ibid.

30. Rachel Benson Gold and Elizabeth Nash, "State Abortion Counseling Policies and the Fundamental Principles of Informed Consent," *Guttmacher Policy Review* 10, no. 4 (Fall 2007), http://www.guttmacher.org/pubs/gpr/10/4/gpr100406.html.

31. Carole Joffe, *Dispatches from the Abortion Wars: The Costs of Fanaticism to Doctors, Patients, and the Rest of Us* (Boston: Beacon Press, 2009), 49.

32. Michelle Alexander, *The New Jim Crow: Mass Incarceration in the Age of Colorblindness* (New York: The New Press, 2010), 6.

33. William Saletan, *Bearing Right: How Conservatives Won the Abortion War* (Berkeley: University of California Press: 2004), 22.

34. Ibid.

35. Ibid., 119.

36. Silliman et al., *Undivided Rights*, 31.

37. Saletan, *Bearing Right*, 41.

38. Ibid., 43.

39. Ibid., 60.

40. Ibid., 56.

41. Nash et al., *Laws Affecting Reproductive Health and Rights*.

42. "A New Vision for Advancing Our Movement for Reproductive Health, Reproductive Rights, and Reproductive Justice," Asian Communities for Reproductive Justice (now called Forward Together), 2005, http://forwardtogether.org/assets/docs/ACRJ-A-New-Vision.pdf.

43. Emily Bazelon, "Is There a Post-Abortion Syndrome?" *New York Times Magazine*, January 21, 2007, http://www.nytimes.com/2007/01/21/magazine/21abortion.t.html?pagewanted=all&_r=1&.

44. Ibid.

45. Ibid.

46. Ibid.

47. Nancy Adler et al., "Psychological responses after abortion," *Science* 248 (1990), 41–44, http://www.sciencemag.org/content/248/4951/41.

48. Nada L. Stotland, MD, "The Myth of the Abortion Trauma Syndrome," *Journal of the American Medical Association* 268, no. 15 (1992), 2078–79.

49. In 2008, researchers at the Johns Hopkins Bloomberg School of Public Health published their own analysis: "The highest-quality research available does not support the hypothesis that abortion leads to long-term mental health problems" (http://www.jhsph.edu/research/centers-and-institutes/center-for-adolescent-health/_includes/Charles_2008_Contraception.pdf). They found a "clear

trend" indicating that "the highest quality studies had findings that were mostly neutral, suggesting few, if any, differences between women who had abortions and their respective comparison groups in terms of mental health sequelae." Notably, the Johns Hopkins teams found that it was the "studies with the most flawed methodology [that] found negative mental health sequelae of abortion." And Susan Cohen summarized the scientific and political landscape for the Spring 2013 *Guttmacher Policy Review*: "In the last five years alone, at least three more major reports reached similar conclusions. In 2006, the APA revisited the issue and created another task force on mental health and abortion. Its updated and comprehensive report, issued in 2008, reinforced its findings from two decades earlier: 'The best scientific evidence published indicates that among adult women who have an *unplanned pregnancy* the relative risk of mental health problems is no greater if they have a single elective first-trimester abortion than if they deliver that pregnancy.'"

Chapter 3, Listen and Tell Stories

1. Joffe, *Dispatches from the Abortion Wars*, xv.

2. Tracy Weitz, "The morning after: A reflection on 'No Easy Decision,'" *ANSIRH Blog*, December 29, 2010, http://blog.ansirh.org/2010/12/reflection-on-16andpregnant/.

3. Carol Hanish, "The Personal Is Political," http://www.carolhanisch.org/CHwritings/PIP.html.

4. Ibid.

5. Ibid.

6. Piecing It Together: Feminism and Nonviolence, Feminism and Nonviolence Study Group, http://www.wri-irg.org/pubs/Feminism_and_Nonviolence.

7. Ibid.

8. Ibid.

9. Ibid.

10. Ta-Nehisi Coates, "Mandela and the Question of Violence," *Atlantic*, December 11, 2013, http://www.theatlantic.com/politics/archive/2013/12/mandela-and-the-question-of-violence/282255/.

11. Ibid.

12. Steph Herold, "Using video to de-stigmatize abortion: An interview with Katie Gillum," *ANSIRH Blog*, October 25, 2013, http://blog.ansirh.org/2013/10/using-video-to-destigmatize-abortion/.

13. Tracy Weitz, "What do responses to the Washington DC 20-week abortion ban tell us about the habits of the prochoice movement?" *ANSIRH Blog*, July 25, 2012, http://blog.ansirh.org/2012/07/habits-of-the-prochoice-movement/.

14. Herold, "Using video to de-stigmatize abortion."

15. Alexander, *The New Jim Crow*, 227.

16. Ibid.

17. Chimamanda Ngozi Adichie, "The danger of a single story," TEDGlobal 2009, filmed July 2009, http://www.ted.com/talks/chimamanda_adichie_the_danger_of_a_single_story.html.

18. Jozen Cummings, "Men Recall the Pain and Turmoil of Abortion," *Root*, November 25, 2013, http://www.theroot.com/articles/politics/2013/11/his_side_a_man_s_perspective_on_abortion.html.

19. Liz Welch, "How Our Abortion Changed Our Relationship," *Cosmopolitan*, January 21, 2014, http://www.cosmopolitan.com/sex-love/advice/a18929/how-abortion-changed-our-relationship/.

20. I'mNotSorry.net, http://www.imnotsorry.net/.

21. Silent No More Awareness, http://www.silentnomoreawareness.org/.

22. Anonymous, "My Abortion, Their Political Ploy," *Salon*, April 13, 2010, http://www.salon.com/2010/04/13/abortion_executive_order/.

23. Ibid.

24. Catharine Smith and Bianca Bosker, "Angie Jackson's Abortion on Twitter: Woman Live-Tweets Her Miscarriage," *Huffington Post*, April 29, 2010, http://www.huffingtonpost.com/2010/02/27/angie-jackson-abortion-tw_n_478495.html.

25. Nelle-Yecats, comment on "Angie Jackson's Abortion on Twitter: Woman Live-Tweets Her Miscarriage," *HuffPost Social News*, http://www.huffingtonpost.com/social/Nelle-Yecats?action=comments.

26. Twitter.com, @abortioneers, April 22, 2010. I expanded the 140-character tweet limit to make her comment more readable.

27. Hanna Rosin, *The End of Men: And the Rise of Women* (New York: Riverhead Books, 2012), 14–15.

28. Jennifer Homans, "A Woman's Place," review of *The End of Men: And the Rise of Women*, *New York Times*, September 13, 2012, http://www .nytimes.com/2012/09/16/books/review/the-end-of-men-by-hanna-rosin.html?pagewanted=all.

29. Erick Erickson, "Reality Check," *RedState* (blog), http://www.red-state.com/ 2013/07/11/reality-check-2/.

30. Ibid.

31. RobtheIdealist, "Are You Tired of the Social Justice Outrage Machine?" *Orchestrated Pulse* (blog), January 6, 2014, http://www.orchestrated-pulse.com/2014/01/tired-social-justice-outrage-machine/.

32. Welch, "How Our Abortion Changed Our Relationship."

33. Adam Liptak, "The Polarized Court," *New York Times*, May 10, 2014, http://www.nytimes.com/2014/05/11/upshot/the-polarized-court .html?_r=0.

34. Christy Wampole, "In Praise of Disregard," *New York Times*, February 16, 2014, http://opinionator.blogs.nytimes.com/2014/02/16/in-praise-of-disregard/?_r=0.

35. Sally Kohn, "Let's Try Emotional Correctness," TED.com, filmed October 13, 2013, http://www.ted.com/talks/sally_kohn_let_s_try_emotional_correctness

36. Larry Kramer, "Tackling Political Polarization Through Philanthropy," *Stanford Social Innovation Review*, December 5, 2013, http://www .ssireview.org/blog/entry/tackling_political_polarization_through_philanthropy.

37. Anna Holmes, "Maybe You Should Read the Book: The Sheryl Sandberg Backlash," *New Yorker*, March 4, 2013, http://www.newyorker .com/online/blogs/books/2013/03/maybe-you-should-read-the-book-the-sheryl-sandberg-backlash.html.

38. Anne-Marie Slaughter, "Why Women Still Can't Have It All," *Atlantic*, July/August 2012, http://www.theatlantic.com/magazine/archive/2012/07/why-women-still-cant-have-it-all/309020/.

39. Maggie Haberman, "Hillary Clinton Advice to Women: Thick Skin," *Politico*, February 13, 2014, http://www.politico.com/story/2014/02/hillary-clinton-advice-to-women-nyu-103505.html.

40. Melissa Harris-Lacewell, address to guests of Planned Parenthood of San Diego and Riverside counties, YouTube, uploaded June 8, 2009, http://www.youtube.com/watch?v=QXiJ_bOFKY8.

41. Francesca Polletta, *It Was Like a Fever: Storytelling in Protest and Politics* (Chicago: University of Chicago Press, 2006), 176.

42. Ibid.

43. Francesca Polletta, sociology professor, University of California, Irvine, phone conversation with the author, 2012.

44. Mira Ptacin, "Un-bearing," *Guernica*, March 1, 2012, http://www.guernicamag.com/features/ptacin_3_1_12/.

45. Polletta, phone conversation.

46. Polletta, *It Was Like a Fever*, 128.

47. Polletta, phone conversation.

48. Sam Gregory, program director, WITNESS, phone conversation with the author, 2012.

Chapter 4, Embrace Gray Areas

1. Steve Pinker, *The Better Angels of Our Nature: Why Violence Has Declined* (New York: Penguin Press, 2011).

2. Gordon Wood, *The Radicalism of the American Revolution* (New York: Random House, 1993), 186.

3. Ibid., 5.

4. Ibid., 95.

5. Ibid., 232.

6. Ibid., 220.

7. Ibid., 221.

8. Ibid., 222.

9. Taylor Branch, *At Canaan's Edge: America in the King Years 1965–68* (New York: Simon & Schuster, 2006), xi.

10. Ibid.

11. Ibid., 25.

12. Paul Tullis, "Can Forgiveness Play a Role in Criminal Justice?" *New York Times*, January 4, 2013, http://www.nytimes.com/2013/01/06/magazine/can-forgiveness-play-a-role-in-criminal-justice.html?pagewanted=all&_r=0.

13. Bazelon, "Is There a Post-Abortion Syndrome?"

14. Rush Limbaugh, "Post-Abortion E-Cards Offered for Women," *Rush Limbaugh Show*, March 14, 2007, http://www.rushlimbaugh.com/daily/2007/03/14/post_abortion_e_cards_offered_for_women.

15. Carol Lloyd, "Abortion e-cards: 'Healing is possible. May you find peace after your abortion'? Oy," Salon.com, March 15, 2007, http://www.salon.com/2007/03/15/abortion_cards/.

16. AbortionChangesYou.com, http://www.abortionchangesyou.com/healing pathways.

17. Ibid.

18. Saletan, *Bearing Right*.

19. Katie J. M. Baker, "Planned Parenthood Steers Clear of 'Choice' and 'Life,'" *Jezebel*, January 10, 2013, http://jezebel.com/5974798/planned-parenthood-steers-clear-of-choice-and-life.

20. Michael Hirschorn, "The Enduring, Multigenerational Appeal of Justin Timberlake," *New York Times Style Magazine*, September 12, 2013, http://tmagazine.blogs.nytimes.com/2013/09/12/the-enduring-multigenerational-appeal-of-justin-timberlake/?_r=0.

21. Baker, "Planned Parenthood Steers Clear of 'Choice' and 'Life.'"

22. Lisa Lepson, "Losing Ownership of New Ideas: A Mark of Success," *Stanford Social Innovation Review Blog*, April 29, 2013, http://www.ssireview.org/blog/entry/losing_ownership_of_new_ideas_a_mark_of_success.

23. Ibid.

24. For more information about Exhale's "16 and Loved" campaign, read the full case study by Deanna Zandt, http://www.deannazandt.com/2011/02/25/case-study-in-social-media-for-social-justice-exhales-16-loved-campaign/.

25. *No Easy Decision*, MTV, December 28, 2010, http://www.mtv.com/
videos/no-easy-decision-special/1654990/playlist.jhtml.

26. Jamia Wilson, "MTV Abortion Special 'No Easy Decision' Addresses
Abortion with Compassionate Integrity," *Women's Media Center Blog*,
December 29, 2010, http://www.womensmediacenter.com/blog/
entry/mtv-abortion-special-no-easy-decision-addresses-abortion-with-
compassionate.

27. Jessica Valenti, "MTV's Abortion Special Treats Issue with Compassion, Facts," Jessica Valenti.com, December 29, 2010, https://
www.facebook.com/permalink.php?story_fbid=152240691491939
&id=360994083159.

28. Shoshanna Walter, "Post-Abortion Counseling Group Finds
Itself on the Firing Line," *New York Times*, January 14, 2011,
http://www.nytimes.com/2011/01/14/us/14bcexhale.html?
pagewanted=2&_r=4&ref=sanfran.

29. Jennifer Armstrong, "Is Abortion No Longer Taboo for TV?" *Entertainment Weekly*, October 12, 2010, http://popwatch.ew.com/2010/10/12/
abortion-mad-men-friday-night-lights/.

30. Eyal Rabinovitch, "Can Listening to Women Who Have Had Abortions Bring Peace to the Abortion Wars?" *Exhale*, May 3, 2010, http://
exhaleisprovoice.files.wordpress.com/2010/05/exhalepeacepaper
byerabinovitch5-3-10.pdf.

Chapter 5, Shape What's Next

1. The first meeting between Joan Blades and Mark Meckler was covered by the *San Francisco Chronicle*: Joe Garofoli, "MoveOn founder,
Tea Party figure meet," January 17, 2013, http://www.sfgate.com/
politics/joegarofoli/article/MoveOn-founder-Tea-Party-figure-
meet-4204384.php. Blades' organization Living Room Conversations
is a structured format for conversation that anyone can use. Learn
more at http://www.livingroomconversations.org/.

2. Daniel M. Haybron, "Happiness and Its Discontents," *New York Times*,
April 13, 2014, http://opinionator.blogs.nytimes.com/2014/04/13/
happiness-and-its-discontents/.

3. Ibid.

4. Jason Marsh and Jill Suttie, "Is a Happy Life Different from a Meaningful One?" Greater Good Science Center, University of California, Berkeley, February 25, 2014, http://greatergood.berkeley.edu/article/item/happy_life_different_from_meaningful_life.

5. Ibid.

6. Emily Esfahani Smith and Jennifer L. Aaker, "Millennial Searchers," *New York Times*, November 30, 2013, http://www.nytimes.com/2013/12/01/opinion/sunday/millennial-searchers.html.

7. Marsh and Suttie, "Is a Happy Life Different from a Meaningful One?"

8. His Holiness the Dalai Lama, *The Art of Happiness* (London: Hodder & Stoughton, 1998).

9. Gloria Steinem, "Gloria Steinem: Why Our Revolution Has Just Begun," *Ms. Magazine*, February 27, 2014, http://msmagazine.com/blog/2014/02/27/gloria-steinem-why-our-revolution-has-just-begun/.

10. Barash and Lipton, *Payback*, 75.

11. Laura Hudson, "Why You Should Think Twice Before Shaming Anyone on Social Media," *Wired*, July 24, 2013, http://www.wired.com/2013/07/ap_argshaming/.

12. Michelle Goldberg, "Feminism's Toxic Twitter Wars," *Nation*, January 29, 2014, http://www.thenation.com/article/178140/feminisms-toxic-twitter-wars?page=0,0.

13. Ibid.

14. Barash and Lipton, *Payback*, 98.

15. Ta Nehisi Coates, "'In God We Trust—but We Have Put Our Faith in Our Guns,'" *Atlantic*, February 3, 2014, http://www.theatlantic.com/politics/archive/2014/02/in-god-we-trust-but-we-have-put-our-faith-in-our-guns/283534/.

16. Tal Kopan, "Glenn Beck recalls 'awful lot of mistakes,'" *Politico*, January 22, 2014, http://www.politico.com/story/2014/01/glenn-beck-fox-news-102464.html#ixzz2tzDDswC4.

17. M. K. Gandhi, *India of My Dreams* (Ahmedabad, India: Navajivan Publishing House, 2001).

18. Barash and Lipton, *Payback*, 163–97.

19. Branch, *At Canaan's Edge*, 240.

20. Daniel Smith, "It's the End of the World as We Know It . . . and He Feels Fine," *New York Times Magazine*, April 17, 2014, http://www .nytimes.com/2014/04/20/magazine/its-the-end-of-the-world-as-we-know-it-and-he-feels-fine.html?ref=magazine.

21. Raven Brooks, executive director, Netroots Nation, phone conversation with the author, November 2013.

22. King, *A Testament of Hope*, 584.

23. Eveline Shen, executive director, Forward Together, phone conversation with the author, December 2013.

24. Brooks, phone conversation.

25. Shen, phone conversation.

26. King, *A Testament of Hope*, 555.

27. Shen, phone conversation.

28. Akaya Windwood, executive director, Rockwood Leadership Institute, phone conversation with the author, December 2013.

29. Shira Saperstein, former deputy director, the Moriah Fund, phone conversation with the author, December 2013.

30. Kirsten Moore, former president and CEO, the Reproductive Health Technologies Project, phone conversation with the author, November 15, 2013.

31. Windwood, phone conversation.

32. For more information about listening, please check out Exhale's Pro-Voice Counseling Guide: https://exhaleprovoice.org/feature/pro-voice-counseling-guide.

33. For more information about storytelling, please check out Exhale's Ethical Storytelling Resources: https://exhaleprovoice.org/ethical-storysharing.

34. Shen, phone conversation.

35. For more information about self-care, please check out Exhale's Self-Care Resources: https://exhaleprovoice.org/self-care.

36. Alexander, *The New Jim Crow*, 234.

37. Chloe Johnson, "Meet Devonte, the little boy with a big heart," *Paper Trail*, November 10, 2014, http://www.papertrail.co.nz/ meet-devonte-little-boy-big-heart/.

Conclusion

1. Nick Shore, "Millennials: The new American dreamers," HLN, November 14, 2012, http://www.hlntv.com/article/2012/11/14/ nick-shore-mtv-gen-y-millennial-making-america.

2. Meg James, "MTV remakes itself for the millennial generation," *Los Angeles Times*, October 2, 2011, http://articles.latimes.com/2011/ oct/02/entertainment/la-ca-mtv-research-20111002.

3. Sheila Marikar, "For Millennials, a Generational Divide," *New York Times*, December 20, 2013, www.nytimes.com/2013/12/22/fashion/ Millenials Millennials-Generation-Y.html.

Resources

Exhale Services and Resources

Exhale

https://exhaleprovoice.org

Exhale's After-Abortion Talkline

https://exhaleprovoice.org/after-abortion-talkline
Call Exhale to talk freely about your experience with abortion. The talkline is toll-free and available throughout the United States:
1-866-4-EXHALE (1-866-439-4253)
Monday–Friday, 5–10 p.m. Pacific time
Saturday–Sunday, noon–10 p.m. Pacific time
If you live outside of the United States, you can call 510-446-7977.

Pro-Voice Counseling Guide

https://exhaleprovoice.org/feature/pro-voice-counseling guide
This guide collects much of what Exhale has learned about supporting emotional wellbeing after an abortion and how to practice being pro-voice.

Self-Care Guide

https://exhaleprovoice.org/self-care
Tips on paying attention to physical, mental, and emotional needs after an abortion, and proactively taking steps to meet those needs.

Talkline Caller Feedback

https://exhaleprovoice.org/tell-us-about-your-call
Have you called Exhale and spoken to a counselor? Share feedback on your call.

Talkline Volunteering

https://exhaleprovoice.org/volunteer
Effective, compassionate listeners and skilled communicators are needed for Exhale's award-winning national talkline. Become a pro-voice talkline counselor.

Join the Pro-Voice Conversation

Stay in touch on Facebook and Twitter:
http://www.facebook.com/ExhaleProVoice
http://twitter.com/exhaleprovoice

Read the Pro-Voice blog:
https://exhaleprovoice.org/blog

Share your story:

https://exhaleprovoice.org/shareyourstory

- Add Your Voice
  Share your story anonymously with others who have had
  personal abortion experiences on Exhale's website.

- A Guide to Publicly Sharing Your Story
  https://exhaleprovoice.org/guide-publicly-sharing-your-story

- A Storysharing Guide for Ethical Advocates
  https://exhaleprovoice.org/storysharing-guide-ethical-advocates

**Sign the Pro-Voice Pledge—Help create more supportive
conversations about abortion:**
https://exhaleprovoice.org/sign-pro-voice-pledge

**Take Our Listening Quiz—Five questions that provide tried-and-true
tips to be a pro listener for the people who need you:**
https://exhaleprovoice.org/take-our-listening-quiz

**Watch a trailer for the *Pro-Voice Project*, a documentary film about
Exhale's 2013 storysharing tour:**
https://exhaleprovoice.org/provoicefilm

Check out the Pro-Voice FAQs:
https://exhaleprovoice.org/top-5-questions-about-pro-voice

Abortion Support Services and Resources

Backline

http://yourbackline.org

1-888-493-0092

Monday–Thursday, 5–10 p.m. Pacific time

Friday–Sunday, 10 a.m.–3 p.m. Pacific time

Backline promotes unconditional and judgment-free support for people in all their decisions, feelings and experiences with pregnancy, parenting, adoption and abortion.

Connect & Breathe

connectandbreathe.org

1-866-647-1764

Tuesdays and Thursdays, 6–9 p.m. Eastern time

Saturdays, 10 a.m.–2 p.m. Eastern time

Connect & Breathe creates safe space to talk about abortion experiences by offering a talkline providing unbiased support and encouragement of self-care.

The Doula Project

www.doulaproject.org

Provides free compassionate care and emotional, physical, and informational support to people across the spectrum of pregnancy.

Experiencing Abortion: A Weaving of Women's Words

By Eve Kushner (Routledge, 1997)

Faith Aloud

www.faithaloud.org

1-888-717-5010

Faith Aloud supports reproductive freedom for every person. Persons of any religious faith are equally welcome to receive services from trained counselors of diverse faith backgrounds, including Roman Catholic, Jewish, Buddhist, Protestant, and more.

The Healing Choice: Your Guide to Emotional Recovery After an Abortion

By Candace De Puy, PhD, MSW, and Dana Dovitch, PhD, MFCC (Fireside, 1997)

A Heartbreaking Choice

aheartbreakingchoice.net

Supports women and men who have terminated a pregnancy specifically for medical reasons. Includes private forums, an e-mail list to connect with others who have had similar experiences, memorial ideas, and suggestions for healing.

Hope Clinic for Women

hopeclinic.com

Offers many pamphlets on a range of issues for women and men after an abortion.

Mayo Clinic

www.mayoclinic.org

Medically accurate information about a range of women's health topics online.

National Abortion Federation

prochoice.org

For financial information and general information about abortion, call 1-800-772-9100.

Monday–Friday, 8 a.m.–11 p.m. Eastern time

Saturdays, 9 a.m.–9 p.m. Eastern time

For referrals to quality abortion providers or to report any issues with providers, call 1-877-257-0012.

Monday–Friday, 9 a.m.–9 p.m. Eastern time

Saturdays, 9 a.m.–5 p.m. Eastern time

Peace After Abortion

peaceafterabortion.com

Planned Parenthood Foundation of America

www.plannedparenthood.org

1-800-230-7526 (PLAN); 24 hours; English and Spanish

Pregnancy Options Workbook

pregnancyoptions.info

Radical Doula

radicaldoula.com

Culture Change Resources

1 in 3 Campaign
www.1in3campaign.org

The Abortion Conversation Project
abortionconversation.com

Abortion Diary
theabortiondiarypodcast.com

Living Room Conversations
www.livingroomconversations.org

Project Voice
www.projectvoice.org

The Sea Change Program
seachangeprogram.org

Strong Families (an initiative of Forward Together)
http://strongfamiliesmovement.org/

Additional Resources for Health and Wellbeing

2-1-1
211search.org
Provides resources for issues of homelessness, poverty, health insurance, counseling services, employment support, child care, etc.

American Psychological Association (APA) Psychologist Locator
locator.apa.org

ANAD (National Association of Anorexia Nervosa and Associated Disorders)
www.anad.org
Offers phone and e-mail support, regional support groups, and related services and information for individuals and families regarding prevention and alleviation of eating disorders.

Boys Town National Hotline

www.boystown.org

1-800-448-3000; 24 hours; English, Spanish, and translation services
Crisis, resource, and referral line for teens and parents with any
concern (suicide, depression, parental stress, school issues, domestic
violence, substance abuse, and more).

First Candle

www.firstcandle.org

1-800-221-7437; English and Spanish

24 hours a day, seven days a week

Offers support services to ensure that grieving families receive
compassionate grief support and have access to the most current
information and materials when the loss of a baby occurs.

GLBT National Help Center

glbtnationalhelpcenter.org

GLBT National Hotline: 1-888-843-4564

GLBT National Youth Talkline: 1-800-246-7743

Monday–Friday, 1–9 p.m. Pacific time

Saturday, 9 a.m.–2 p.m. Pacific time

Provides telephone and e-mail peer counseling services around
coming-out issues, relationship concerns, HIV/AIDS anxiety,
safer-sex information, etc.

Mental Health America

mentalhealthamerica.net/faqs

Comprehensive information about a wide range of mental health
topics and disorders.

National Domestic Violence Hotline

www.thehotline.org

Call toll-free 1-800-799-SAFE (7233)

24 hours a day, seven days a week

National Sexual Assault Hotline

https://rainn.org

Call toll-free 1-800-656-4673

24 hours a day, seven days a week

National Suicide Prevention Lifeline

www.suicidepreventionlifeline.org

1-800-273-TALK (8255); 24 hours; English (other languages vary)

1-888-628-9454; 24 hours; Spanish

1-800-799-4TTY (4889); 24 hours; TTY

Automatically connects you to your closest certified crisis
center. Trained crisis center staff are available to listen to your
needs and offer crisis counseling, suicide intervention, and mental
health referral information.

Scarleteen

www.scarleteen.com

Sex information for the real world.

Sex, Etc.

sexetc.org

Sex education by teens, for teens.

Substance Abuse and Mental Health Services Administration

Substance Abuse and Mental Health Services Administration

www.samhsa.gov

1-800-662-4357; 24 hours; English, Spanish

For help finding the nearest drug and alcohol abuse and mental

health treatment programs.

Acknowledgments

I'm deeply grateful to the following people for their years of personal support and for being great champions of Exhale: Margot Kramer Biehle, Mardi Kildebeck, Kirsten Moore, Karen Grove, Rebekah Saul Butler, Eveline Shen, Aimee Thorne-Thomsen, Elizabeth Arndorfer, Fran Jemmott, Saba Brelvi, Shira Saperstein, Tom Layton, Lourdes Rivera, Peter Belden, Lana Dakan, Ellen Friedman, Tracy Salkowitz, Thaler Pekar, Lisa Hoffman, Susan Chorley, and Danielle Thomas. I honor Exhale's history of tremendous board chairs, whom I love dearly: Lisa Lepson, Jennifer Rudy, Kristin Rothballer, and Jocelyn Yin.

I appreciate every person who has made Exhale a better, stronger organization through their leadership as a board or staff member; or as a talkline counselor, fellow, ambassador, donor, or volunteer; or as a coach or consultant. I wish I could list you all here, but you know who you are! I thank my cofounders for their desire to support women postabortion, among them Carolina De Robertis, who cowrote the very first white paper on pro-voice with me.

To all the unsung champions of Exhale and pro-voice, the risks you've been willing to take to open conversations and support women postabortion is inspiring. In particular, I applaud Rachel Falls, Lynne Randall, and Kathy Kneer for their leadership.

Rich Snowdon and Michelle Gislason: You taught me exactly what I needed, when I needed it most, and I've been learning from you ever since. Your wisdom has infused my leadership, Exhale, pro-voice, and this book, and I'm deeply grateful for your teaching.

Thank you to my research assistant, Susan Haskell Khan, for delivering interesting and insightful commentary and thorough history on a wide range of topics in very short periods of time. Susannah Gardner, your humor made your edits easier to take.

Thank you to the Peace and Conflict Studies department at the University of California, Berkeley, and its former chair Jerry Sanders, for encouraging me to put forward my own unique ideas for how to resolve conflict and create peace.

Thank you to the Mesa Refuge—especially its founder, Peter Barnes, and executive director, Susan Page Tillett, for their encouragement and the time and space to finish the book in beautiful Point Reyes, California.

And to Neal Maillet and Jeevan Sivasubramaniam at Berrett-Koehler: You've been terrific editors, champions, and truth tellers. You've helped make the whole process of writing this book one of the best experiences of my life. I've loved every minute. Thank you.

To my family and friends, thank you for helping me cultivate happiness and joy in my life.

Index

About the Author

Aspen Baker is the leading voice in the nation on how to transform the abortion conflict. She was a finalist for the 2014 American Express NGen Leadership Awards; was called a "fun, fearless female" by *Cosmopolitan* in 2013; was awarded the Gerbode Professional Development Fellowship in 2012; was named a "Women's History Hero" in 2009 by San Francisco's KQED during Women's History Month; and was named "Young Executive Director of the Year" in 2005 by the Bay Area's Young Nonprofit Professionals Network. Aspen served on the City of Oakland's Public Ethics Commission 2011–2014. As a spokesperson for Exhale, she has been featured by media outlets across the country, among them CNN *Headline News*, *Fox National News*, *Ladies' Home Journal*, *Cosmopolitan*, *Glamour*, the *New York Times*, National Public Radio, *Newsweek*, the *New Republic*, Alternet, and *Bust*. Her essay "My Abortion Brought Us Together" was included in the anthology *Nothing but the Truth So Help Me God: 51 Women Reveal the Power of Positive Female Connection*. She often writes for sites like the *Stanford Social Innovation Review* and *Huffington Post*. Aspen is a graduate of UC Berkeley, and she lives in Oakland, California, with her family. Twitter: @aspenbaker.

Berrett–Koehler
Publishers

Berrett-Koehler is an independent publisher dedicated to an ambitious mission: *Creating a World That Works for All*.

We believe that to truly create a better world, action is needed at all levels—individual, organizational, and societal. At the individual level, our publications help people align their lives with their values and with their aspirations for a better world. At the organizational level, our publications promote progressive leadership and management practices, socially responsible approaches to business, and humane and effective organizations. At the societal level, our publications advance social and economic justice, shared prosperity, sustainability, and new solutions to national and global issues.

A major theme of our publications is "Opening Up New Space." Berrett-Koehler titles challenge conventional thinking, introduce new ideas, and foster positive change. Their common quest is changing the underlying beliefs, mindsets, institutions, and structures that keep generating the same cycles of problems, no matter who our leaders are or what improvement programs we adopt.

We strive to practice what we preach—to operate our publishing company in line with the ideas in our books. At the core of our approach is stewardship, which we define as a deep sense of responsibility to administer the company for the benefit of all of our "stakeholder" groups: authors, customers, employees, investors, service providers, and the communities and environment around us.

We are grateful to the thousands of readers, authors, and other friends of the company who consider themselves to be part of the "BK Community." We hope that you, too, will join us in our mission.

A BK Currents Book

This book is part of our BK Currents series. BK Currents books advance social and economic justice by exploring the critical intersections between business and society. Offering a unique combination of thoughtful analysis and progressive alternatives, BK Currents books promote positive change at the national and global levels. To find out more, visit **www.bkconnection.com**.

Berrett–Koehler
Publishers

A community dedicated to creating
a world that works for all

Dear Reader,

Thank you for picking up this book and joining our worldwide community of Berrett-Koehler readers. We share ideas that bring positive change into people's lives, organizations, and society.

To welcome you, we'd like to offer you a free e-book. You can pick from among twelve of our bestselling books by entering the promotional code BKP92E here: http://www.bkconnection.com/welcome.

When you claim your free e-book, we'll also send you a copy of our e-newsletter, the *BK Communiqué*. Although you're free to unsubscribe, there are many benefits to sticking around. In every issue of our newsletter you'll find

- A free e-book
- Tips from famous authors
- Discounts on spotlight titles
- Hilarious insider publishing news
- A chance to win a prize for answering a riddle

Best of all, our readers tell us, "Your newsletter is the only one I actually read." So claim your gift today, and please stay in touch!

Sincerely,

Charlotte Ashlock
Steward of the BK Website

Questions? Comments? Contact me at bkcommunity@bkpub.com.